To Susan,

Happy Nursing Week!

From,

Shadonne

A Gift of Hope

52 Ways to Live a Better Life

Shadonna Richards, R.N.

Copyright © 2008 by Shadonna Richards

ISBN 0-7414-5167-0

Published by:

INFINITY
PUBLISHING.COM

1094 New DeHaven Street, Suite 100
West Conshohocken, PA 19428-2713
Info@buybooksontheweb.com
www.buybooksontheweb.com
Toll-free (877) BUY BOOK
Local Phone (610) 941-9999
Fax (610) 941-9959

Printed in the United States of America

Printed on Recycled Paper

Published December 2008

Dedicated in loving memory
To my brother Rodney Richards aka DJ Rodric (1980-2000)
Such talent. Such potential.
You were gone too soon.

And to my great grandmother Estina Myrina Whitter
(1889-1994).
Your wisdom, your courage, your inner-strength and grace
will forever live in my heart.

To Solomon

"Where there is life, there is hope."

--Publius Terentius Afer (Terence)
(195 BC—159 BC)

CONTENTS

About the Author

Shadonna Richards is a freelance writer, former newspaper columnist and registered nurse. She is the author of more than 250 newspaper articles and inspirational stories. Her work has appeared in various publications including *The Toronto Star, Toronto Sun, Word Magazine, Scarborough Mirror* and *Metro Newspaper*. She also has a Bachelor of Arts Degree in Psychology and lives in Canada with her husband and son.

In the spirit of promoting mental health and well being, Shadonna will donate a portion of the proceeds from this book to the Canadian Mental Health Association. Also, a portion of the proceeds will go towards finding a cure for cancer.

You may contact Shadonna by e-mail at shadonna@ymail.com or visit her MySpace page at *www.myspace.com/shadonnarichards*

Acknowledgments

First and foremost, thank You, God, for Your divine guidance, the gift of life, providing me the ability to write so that I can share my experiences with others and for everything I've been blessed with in my life.

Thanks to everyone who has participated in this project. It has been a privilege to write and compile my previously published newspaper columns and inspirational articles profiling amazing individuals.

I am thankful for all the wonderful readers of my columns and articles and the letters received in response to the stories published and all the amazing people I've interviewed for my articles—too many to name. I interviewed many in the early stages of their careers and dreams who have gone on to flourish and continue to bless others.

To the associations for their help in my research—too many to name but inclusive of the Canadian Mental Health Association, Heart and Stroke Foundation of Canada, and the Canadian Cancer Society.

Special thanks to the leaders, philosophers, speakers and all those whom I've quoted for their words of wisdom.

To the wonderful patients for whom I've had the honor of working. To the great team of colleagues with whom I've had the pleasure of working.

To Sheldon Burshtein, LLB, for answering my questions pertaining to copyright law and Debbie Macina for the referral.

To all the talented editors with whom I am grateful to have worked with, especially Virginia Somersall, R.N. and Marielle Marne.

To my peer reviewers who generously donated their time to reading sample chapters from the early draft of the book (in order of reviews received): Laurene Boynton, RN, Dr. Allan Somersall, MD, PhD, Fennella Bruce, Bev Katz Rosenbaum, Alfredo Alleyne, RN, Sandra Martin, Patricia Murphy Kane, RN, Judith Filman, RN, Mitzie Hunter, MBA and especially to Yvonne Blackwood for taking the time to read my entire manuscript and your boundless words of encouragement.

And most important, a very special heartfelt thanks to all my family and close friends for your continued support and love. Too many to name but inclusive of my wonderful mother, Merdella, and my loving grandparents Nesitta, Godwin, Monica and Percell, and last but not least, to my wonderful husband, Jermaine, and our blessed son.

Introduction

My work as a registered nurse who provides compassionate care to terminally ill cancer patients who are informed they have less than six months to live has had a profound effect on my life. It has taught me to value each blessed moment we have in this life. To not squander time. To tell those we love how we feel. And to express that love by our actions towards them. Every single day.

As a writer, I strongly believe in the power of words. Words empower. They can uplift you. Words motivate. Words can move you to change. The choice is often up to how you internalize them and on what you choose to dwell.

Over the years, I have had the privilege of interviewing countless heroic individuals for my newspaper columns and inspirational news stories. These individuals were ordinary people but had extraordinary courage and were able to make changes in their lives and in the world around them. Based on the responses to my articles (many readers have written letters to me and expressed interest in more inspirational stories such as the ones I've published), I decided to share these inspirational stories with you as part of a dynamic collection of wisdom to encourage you through your own life. I want to motivate you to never give up on your dreams; to reassure you that you too can move forward through your own arduous times; to persuade you that nothing is impossible. It's true that happiness is a state of mind, and we do have more control over our lives than we give ourselves credit.

I've noticed that many of the happiest people have one trait in common: a Spiritual First Aid kit that may include a dose of hope, a blanket of support (they do not isolate themselves from loved ones), a boost of humor, and spiritual vitamins to take every morning as they greet each new day. Vitamin A for Acceptance of things they cannot change. Vitamin B for Belief in themselves and their abilities to get through any calamity. Vitamin C for remaining Calm during chaos. Vitamin D for Determination. Vitamin E for Eliminating worries from their diet. Vitamin K for Kindness to others and to themselves.

This book is a collection of 52 inspiring stories, thoughts and pearls of wisdom. One for each week of the year. At the end of each chapter is a suggested Hope Initiative to motivate you to implement positive changes in your life. I've also included a Book of Blessings: Personal Hope Journal at the end for you to fill out and reflect on the highlights of your lives and to never forget the aspects that are going right in your lives (especially when things don't go as planned).

I hope you enjoy the written passages on the pages that follow as much as I've enjoyed writing them.

Good health, love and happiness!
Shadonna

Week 1:

Stay Mentally Fit

*Happiness is not the absence of problems
but the ability to deal with them.*

—Jack Brown

We all long to experience the absolute joy of being alive. Yet, in order to achieve true happiness, we need to take greater care of our mental health. This means staying mentally fit despite our circumstances. Roman philosopher Marcus Aurelius once wrote, "The happiness of your life depends on the quality of your thoughts." If we overload our minds with discouraging thoughts, it's unlikely we'll see the beauty of life. If we're not in optimal mental shape, it's difficult to enjoy the experiences in our lives. Whenever trouble strikes, we must abandon feelings of hopelessness, eliminate negative thinking, exercise faith and keep our spirits soaring on the treadmill of optimism.

We've all experienced feelings of despair which frequently occur when we're struck with a torrential downpour of problems, followed by gusts of negative energy that can sweep us off balance when we least expect it—stress at home, politics at work, strain in our relationships or sudden illness. We need practical ways to shield our minds and balance our emotions during these turbulent times. I found it interesting that according to the Canadian Mental Health Association, one in four Canadians express that their workplace is the major contributor of stress and anxiety in their lives, while the American Psychological Association revealed identical statistics for workers in the U.S. who have taken a mental health day off to cope with stress. Imagine that!

In the past, colleagues would often ask me, "How come you're always so happy? Don't you have any problems?" Well, of course, I do. That's silly. I was always taught that as long as you're alive, you're going to face challenges and deal with stress. That's living! It's dealing with these hurdles *effectively* that is the issue. There are times when I'm overloaded with obstacles, but I've learned over the years to not become consumed with pessimistic thoughts. That only magnifies the problem. I've also learned that true happiness comes from within, and there is power in positive thinking. Keeping in mental shape is now one of my top priorities in my day-to-day routine. I try to set aside at least one minute of positive thinking and meditation every chance I get.

Try the following 15 spiritual exercises for managing stress and achieving optimum mental fitness:

Exercise 1. **Identify, then rectify.** A crucial part of any solution is locating the problem. Do worries keep you up at night? Go directly to the source of your tension. Visit the CMHA website at *www.cmha.ca* and take the free online test "What's your stress index?" to help you pinpoint areas in your life that may need attention. You may be surprised! Remember, when dealing with your troubling emotions you must identify the source then seek ways to rectify those issues.

Exercise 2. **Detox your mind.** The term "mental detox" is becoming increasingly popular today. Our minds get polluted every day with negative suggestions and situations—but many of us do nothing to detox our most valuable asset that controls our lives—our minds. We protect our homes, our cars and our other valuables from damage and loss more than our minds. It is the one asset we can't afford to lose. If you had a choice between dwelling on negative thoughts that sink your spirits, and a choice of focusing on thoughts that elevate you and propel you to achieve greatness and enjoy your life, on which would you choose to direct your energies? Most would say the latter. It is that simple. We always have a choice. We can choose to dwell on being hopeless in situations or focus on having hope. I love the saying that there are no hopeless situations, only people who think hopelessly. Choose hope. Choose happiness. Flush out any doubts or negative thoughts by feeding yourself positive thoughts or spiritual words. Be careful not to be consumed with negativity because it can overshadow your thinking and your life. In the morning, go through a spiritual detox regime. Meditate on a scripture or a positive message, mantra, or saying and continue to refuel your soul. As popular televangelist Joel Osteen once said, instead of thinking about what others think of you, dwell on what God (or another higher power) thinks of you, focus on what your loved ones think of you, and most importantly, illuminate the good sentiments you think of yourself.

Exercise 3. **Create Peace of Mind for Yourself.** This may be achieved by setting important contingencies in place. For instance, what would you do in a disaster? Do you have a disaster preparedness kit in place or emergency supplies in your home—just as you would have an emergency kit in your car? Visit *www.redcross.ca* (or *www.redcross.org* outside of Canada) for ideas on how to build a disaster preparedness kit or purchase one from them. What would you do if you were to experience a change in your employment status? Do you have at least three months of living expenses socked away, just in case? Are you adequately covered by insurance? It's nice to have peace of mind in scenarios such as these. We often experience high levels of stress when unforeseen events occur in our lives that disrupt our day-to-day activities and threaten our peace of mind. Set contingencies in place for ease from worrying about how you will cope with a drastic change. It could be something as simple as having backup babysitters to care for your child if your child was home sick from school and you still had to report for work. There's no better frame of mind than peace of mind during chaos.

Exercise 4. **Leave yesterday in the past.** Get rid of that rewind button in your memory of bad situations. I could never understand those who still practice this strange ritual of dwelling on negative occurrences in their past and catapulting their minds and bodies into unnecessary torture as if it will correct the situation. Blessed are those who know how to erase unpleasant moments from their minds. We've all done or said something of which we're not proud. Why let it taunt you? It's gone. Forever. There's a saying, when you think of yesterday without regret and tomorrow without fear, you are near real contentment. Live for the moment.

Exercise 5. **Embrace Hope.** Hope is the driving force that keeps us moving forward in life. It propels us when we are faced with challenges. It is a crucial part of life and our feeling of well-being. Having the belief that a positive outcome is possible despite our circumstances. Hope fuels perseverance and drives us to better ourselves. As Roman philosopher and playwright, Terence, once said, "Where there is life, there is hope." Never give up the belief that things can change. My great-grandmother was given six months to live when diagnosed with cancer in her late seventies. Not only did her disease go into remission but she lived till the advanced age of 105 years with no other health ailments in subsequent years.

Exercise 6. **Focus on solutions; not problems**. See problems as challenges. Don't let your problems *define* you. Let your problems *refine* you. Don't focus on how you've been hurt. Instead, focus on how you can bounce back from the negative situation. Learn from your mistakes. Don't be burned by them. Nothing you have said or done is new under the sun. Everyone who breathes makes mistakes and mistakes typically make us wiser the next time around.

Exercise 7. **Raise Your Confidence Level.** Coach yourself into believing in yourself. Embrace your God-given talents. We all have unique skills and abilities. In fact, it has been said that people are equipped with at least 500 to 800 skills and abilities! We are all capable of doing many things. It could be that you are an exceptional speaker, listener, writer, vocalist, or maybe your congenial nature or charm in addition to technical skills are your crowning glories. Focus on what you are good at and share those gifts with others. There's no better boost for the self-esteem than having accomplishments. Join a club or forum with people who share similar interests. Network. Remember that you are the most important person in your life. Take good care of yourself. If you don't, who will? Why not designate a make-time-for-myself day or moment and meditate or do whatever it is that relaxes you. Give yourself a Happiness Makeover complete with an attitude lift, problem peel and ego massage. Live for the respect of one person in your life. You! What people think about you should not be your prime concern. It's how *you* feel about yourself. You're the one who is living in your skin and will be for decades to come.

Exercise 8. **Laugh**. Laughter has been dubbed the best medicine, time and time again. Have a sense of humor. But remember the saying that it's not just the ability to tell a joke but the ability to take one. Not only is laughter a good muscle relaxant, it also releases endorphins, the body's own "happy drug," into your blood stream. Before anyone else can laugh at you, learn to laugh at yourself when you make a simple mistake. If you are ever at a lost for a good reason to laugh try *www.Google.com* and search for websites on good clean jokes such as *www.ahajokes.com*. This is one of many websites that provide thousands of clean jokes, funny pictures and humorous cartoons.

Exercise 9. **Talk**. It's important to have someone to talk to about your problems or your fears. We need to be able to vent or have a safe outlet to unveil our innermost thoughts. Be cautious though, as you wouldn't want to tell your personal business to the town gossip. If you don't have someone with whom to talk, then why not try the local distress center in your area. As a former crisis-hotline volunteer, I can attest to the effectiveness of such programs. In Toronto, the Distress line is 416-408-HELP (4357), offering 24-hour access to emotional support during difficult times. It is manned by volunteers, is accessible in 151 languages and receives 100,000 calls per year!

Exercise 10. **Change your thoughts.** A person's life is what his or her thoughts make of it. Your life is whatever you focus on. You have the power to choose your moods and control your feelings. Your mind controls your world as you see it. Keep your thoughts favorable especially about yourself. Negative thoughts bring you down and can affect your well-being. Positive thoughts can uplift anyone out of a dark moment. I remember a story I read about 1930s child star, Shirley Temple, who was told by directors to think of something terrible like not seeing her mother again to draw real tears for a scene. This was a technique that actually worked with her. You can see what the power of concentrating on a particular issue can do to our emotions and how it can affect our bodies. If we are feeling down, it is most likely because we are thinking of something that is depressing to us. If negative thoughts enter your mind, switch the "thought" channel and think of something more positive. Or flash the word God or Peace or Love across the window of your mind.

Exercise 11. **Develop Your Own Signature Phrase by which to live.** I've noticed the habits of many optimists who have developed their own signature phrases as their personal anthems. They often reply to negative circumstances by saying: "No worries," "I'm cool," "I'm too blessed to be stressed," "It'll pass," or "I'll get over it," as an antidote to mentally toxic situations—a boost for their spirits. They shrug off any negative situations and are able to move on with their lives. They bounce back quickly when they get knocked down. Develop your own signature phrase or borrow from the above-mentioned examples. The more you tell yourself something—the more you believe it and the more you act on it subconsciously.

Exercise 12. **Pay attention to your overall health**. Make time for yourself to relax. It is very necessary to have balance in your life. All work and no play is counterproductive to your well being. Also, don't forget to exercise. Stay active. You are the most valuable asset you'll ever own. As Dr. Norman Vincent Peale wrote in *The Power of Positive Thinking*, it's important to eliminate the "worry habit" from your spiritual diet. Worry can actually make you ill, so abstain from it. Recharge your emotional batteries often. Eat a well balanced diet according to the Canada Food Guide (or the American Food Pyramid.) In fact visit *www.hc-sc.gc.ca/fn-an/food-guide-aliment/index-eng.php* in Canada or *www.mypyramid.gov* in the US and download a copy of the food guide, get information on a achieving a well balanced diet, set up your own personal exercise guide and create your own personal food guide from these websites.

Exercise 13. **Engage in joyful planning.** In other words, set fun goals for yourself. Whether it is buying a newer car, finding your dream home, adding a new gadget to your collection, finding inner-peace, or taking a much needed vacation. This way, you'll rarely dwell on the obstacles and you're more likely to endure the bad times knowing that something good is coming. Even if it's just looking forward to your days off to relax and unwind or to catch a movie at the cinema. Look forward to something. Anything.

Exercise 14. **Manage Your Relationships:** Forgive those who have done wrong to you. When you forgive—you release toxic thoughts and hurtful emotions and move forward. Cleanse your mind from the bitter residue of past wounds. Forgive yourself as well. None of us are perfect, but we can learn valuable lessons from our mistakes. Appreciate the good in others. When we focus on the good aspects of a person, we tend to think more favorably about them. Accept people as they are. We're not all built the same or express the same interests. Some of us are introverts and some are extroverts. That's okay! In fact, go for a friendship tune-up. When was the last time you really took the time to maintain your relationships? Are there any leaks that need filling? Like gardening, it takes nurturing for relationships to bloom. At the back of this book I've included a fill-in-the-blanks section where you can manage your personal relationships including a calendar to record and remember birthdays. Make time for the people close to you. They say that if you're too busy for family or friends, then you are just too busy. Why not designate Friday or Saturday evening as Family Fun Night? Rent a DVD or go to the theatre. Order take-out. Dine at a fine restaurant. Get into the habit of giving joy to others. As the saying goes, "Happiness is contagious, be a carrier."

Exercise 15. **Have a positive force or motivation driving your life** (whether good people or religion) or you may be driven around to places you may not want to go. And before you believe in anything, or anyone, believe in yourself.

This Week's Hope Initiative:

Start today! Follow some of the aforementioned tips to change your life and your outlook on challenges in your life.

Your Hopes for this Week:

_____

_____

_____

_____

Week 2:

Dare to Dream: Believe that
Anything is Possible

*If there is anyone out there who still doubts America
is a place where all things are possible, who still wonders
if the dream of our founders is alive in our time, who still
questions the power of our democracy—
tonight is your answer.*

—U.S. president-elect Barack Obama

Is there a dream in your heart you secretly wish to become
reality? Is there a path you desire to take in life, but you are
fearful to take the steps necessary in that direction because it
has never been done before?

Well, as the world witnessed on the night of
November 4, 2008, anything is possible! We are living in a
time of infinite hope. A time when we can overcome barriers
to achieve our goals. A time when dreams once deemed
impossible can manifest into reality. Like millions around
the globe, during the early morning hours, I was overcome
with unfiltered joy as I witnessed the dawn of a new era on
November 5, 2008—a day my family, friends and I will
forever remember. A moment of change. A dimension of
possibilities when Illinois Senator Barack Obama made
history as he was elected the first black president of the
United States of America in a landslide victory.

To put things into perspective, 47-year-old Barack
Obama was born during a time of racial segregation when
people of color had to fight for the right to vote. He would
later accomplish the American Dream to lead the nation. He
fulfilled the late civil rights leader, Reverend Martin Luther
King's dream of equality amongst all Americans. Growing

up, I never knew I would live to see the day the United States of America would elect a black president.

Obama's inspirational campaign slogan was "Yes, we can!" What a wonderful expression that quickly changed to "Yes, we did!"

This led us all to believe that any dream is attainable. And yes, it may not have been done before. It may seem impossible or like a long shot, but anything is possible, if we put our hearts, our minds, our actions and our hopes into it.

We can tell our children that regardless of race, color or creed, you can be whatever you desire! Never relinquish hope. Like many parents, I hugged my son, and it felt good to be able to tell him, "Son, you can be whatever you want to be if you put your heart and mind to it." In times of despair, we must embrace those who symbolize hope and remember the monumental moments like the U.S. elections in November 2008 and never forget the changes occurring in the world. Never allow your hope to fade! Possibilities can quickly become realities!

This Week's Hope Initiative:

Believe in the power of possibilities. Believe you can accomplish anything you put your mind to. Believe you can achieve what others may have labeled impossible. Adopt a positive slogan such as "Yes, I can" and work towards changing it to "Yes, I did" like the 44th elected president of the United States. What goals or dreams do you have in your heart? Owning your first home? Becoming president of your own company? Becoming the first in your family to earn a college and/or an advanced degree? What steps will you take towards achieving your dreams?

Your Hopes for this Week:

_____

_____

_____

_____

Week 3:

Make Others Feel Special

*I've learned that people will forget what you said,
people will forget what you did, but people will
never forget how you made them feel.*

—Dr. Maya Angelou

What impressions do you send out to those you meet? Are you pleasant? Kind? Thoughtful? Able to cheer someone up during an overcast moment? Typically the vibes we send out to others transmit back to us in many ways. In many cases, but not all, whatever you give out, you often receive.

One of the first characteristics I noticed about Oprah Winfrey when I initially met her on the set of her TV talk-show was her energetic, positive spirit and unfiltered enthusiasm. She is never at a loss for ways to make others feel special. Her infectious smile and warmth illuminated everyone in the audience. Her high-level motivation and genuine concern for others was palpable. You couldn't be in the same room with Oprah and not be affected by her radiance and good nature. My friend and I who attended the Oprah Show were young university students at the time.

It was the highlight of that semester—getting my name added to the Oprah Winfrey show's ticket reservation list (a tough task to do back then—as it is today). It was December, 1991. The show recording date was December 18. We were not told beforehand what the topic would be, but my friend and I were excited about going to Harpo Studios in Chicago. However, the trip almost didn't happen. The stormy weather was a major factor in deterring us.

Discouraged about going to Chicago during the storm, we were on the verge turning back, but Anne and I decided we should go. We were waiting for two other friends travelling from another university to join us in Windsor before embarking on our travels across the border to Detroit where we could catch the Amtrak train. We later found out that they had difficulty travelling through the snowstorm where they were—this was before cell phones became popular and accessible to everyone. We missed the Amtrak train and were disappointed. I remember we discussed that this was a sign not to go. The blizzard was horrific and left commuters with virtually no visibility. We decided to head out to the Greyhound Bus depot anyway, knowing it would take twice as long to get to Chicago. The trip was atrocious. We travelled in another blizzard through Pennsylvania. The bus was crammed with other riders, including new passengers who hopped on during our stop. I felt closed in and didn't think I could make it. This was before iPods and portable DVD players were available as distractions. We ran out of things to say and were just frustrated.

After Anne and I arrived at the hotel, we clicked on the news and were horrified to see that an Amtrak train had derailed. We both froze, eyes wide open, jaws dropped. Could it be the same train that we were supposed to board? We later discovered it was not the same train we had missed. But we had a strong suspicion we weren't meant to board the train we had missed earlier. We arrived at Harpo Studios the next day extremely tired—trying to push the memory of the eventful journey behind us.

After the taping of the show ended, we were given the opportunity to shake hands and to say hello to Oprah. At first, my then 19-year-old heart was pounding. I'm a huge fan of Oprah's and this was a chance to meet her off-camera. We eagerly lined up behind the other members of the audience and advanced towards the gracious talk-show host. Each person shook hands briefly and moved forward out of the line. The man in front of me deviated from the routine and gave Oprah a good squeeze as he hugged her. I don't know what prompted me, but I reached out to hug her too. As if she was a friend, I explained to her that we came all the way from Canada to see her and the frightening experience we had in getting there. I don't know why I felt compelled to brief her on the terrible time we had in travelling to the show. Oprah was extremely warm, amicable and encouraging. She lit a positive flame by her inviting smile, kind words and positive spirit. Her spiritual glow was contagious. We were feeling glum from the journey but lit up because she was full of light and hope. We forgot about the terrible trip and instead were affected by the light of her enthusiasm. She hugged me again before we left. What an amazing person she is, I thought. Here is the most powerful and popular woman in TV history, and she made two unknown students feel important and special. Oprah's sincerity and kindness had a ripple effect on us.

Later, I told Anne I wanted to be like Oprah. She turned to me with a puzzled expression. I clarified that I wanted to be the type of person that no matter what my position is in life, I will always make people around me feel important. Years later when I ventured into journalism and then nursing, I carried those sentiments with me.

More than anything else, people will always remember you for how you made them feel. How you've shined a light on their overcast moments. You never know how you can affect the life of another by your actions. The feeling of hope that I received after meeting Oprah has stayed with me to this day. It certainly made the trip worthwhile and unforgettable. It has been said that when you give joy to others you cannot keep it from yourself. I believe that is one of the reasons why Oprah is an inspiration to millions. Her success is due in part to the fact that she is natural at spreading joy and encouraging others.

This Week's Hope Initiative:

Whom can you make feel special today? Whom can you offer encouragement to, or a sincere, kind gesture or word? (Hint: It could be a friend or a stranger, a relative, a child, a co-worker or your partner.) List five people and make it a point to make them each feel special.

Your Hopes for this Week:

_____

_____

_____

_____

Week 4:

Be the Friend You Desire to Have

Friendship is God's most precious gift.
—Author Unknown

Be the friend you've always wanted to have to someone else without expecting anything in return. As Gloria Steinem once said, "far too many people are looking *for* the right person, instead of trying to *be* the right person."

We all want someone to listen to our fears, our doubts, help us to problem-solve, get an opinion before we make the next move, to be objective, yet kind, caring, inspirational, funny, to hang out with or go out with. But I find that instead of looking for it in others, it's so much more valuable to give it to others.

People do appreciate having someone who genuinely cares. A good listener, movie-buddy, or simply a companion. You'll feel better and know you are helping others. You also learn more about yourself. When was the last time you told someone she can call you if she needs a listening ear or offered to take someone out to the movies?

Your phone hasn't rung today, but have you rung someone else's phone? Be the friend, the daughter, the sibling, parent, or soul-mate you desire in others. Give the love you want to receive from others. If you want love, give love. If you want joy, give joy. Give it often, expecting nothing in return.

This Week's Hope Initiative:

Whom can you call today? Is there a friend who could use a helping hand? Can you motivate someone today? By expressing genuine kindness to others, we enrich our own lives.

Your Hopes for this Week:

_____

_____

_____

_____

Week 5:

Turn Your Weaknesses Into Your Strengths

The word impossible is not in my dictionary.

—Napoleon Bonaparte

We all have perceived weaknesses. It's a part of being human. We also have strengths and as Ralph Waldo Emerson once said, "our strength grows out of our weaknesses." I wrote a story about Susan, an extraordinary woman who has a disability for my *Scarborough Mirror* column in 1995. She told me that when she was only five-years-old, she developed polio after swimming in a contaminated pool. At that time, the Polish immigrant knew little English and was shunned by schoolmates for being different physically and linguistically. As a child, she had to learn to overcome the cruel treatment of her peers.

But attitude has a lot to do with how your life turns out. She's talented. She's courageous. And she's a woman with boundless positive energy. Susan vowed not to spend the rest of her life depressed about her disability but to focus on her blessings and her inner strength. Today, she is the founder of her own talent agency and believes that "fear will not harm you but fear of success will."

What makes her agency unique is that she specializes in providing actors, models and other talents who are both disabled and able-bodied for movies, television shows and modeling assignments.

"We are a part of society," Susan told me in defense of persons with disabilities being represented in the entertainment industry. "If they're going to depict society (in movies), we should be part of it."

But for her, it's not just a question of plopping a disabled person on the screen when the script calls for it.

31

"We shouldn't be hired just because of our disability," she told me in that interview.

And thanks to this woman of courage and creativity, many persons with disabilities have had great opportunities to unveil their talents in the entertainment industry. Her clients range from a teenager who lost his leg to cancer and played a part in *A Christmas Carol* to a young paraplegic man who played a lawyer on the *New Divorce Court*. She has put clients to work on Levi's, Kellogg's Cornflakes and Bell Canada commercials as well as in various motion pictures.

The talented agent took the initiative to address a need, and through her persistence, she persuaded top ad agencies to use her roster of raw talent to work for them. She paved a way for the physically challenged to have a voice and fulfilled their dreams. She told me she believes that "disability is a state of mind, not a state of being."

This Week's Hope Initiative:

What lesson can you learn from Susan's example? Is there a disability, setback or perceived weakness you feel that's in your way? Try finding ways to use it for your benefit and to reach out to others in similar situations. We all have aspects of our lives that can serve as an inspiration to others.

Your Hopes for this Week:

_____

_____

_____

_____

Week 6:

Keep It Simple

Life is simple, but we insist on making it complicated.

—Confucius

I've always said that life becomes simple when you follow simple rules, and this is what I think:

If you fall down, get back up.
If you get hurt, aim to recover.
If you start to feel down, bounce back up.
If you mess up, clean up.
If you want love, give love.
If you want a friend, be a friend.
If you feel alone, pick up the phone.

If you've been disgraced, move on with grace.
If you've been betrayed, forgive and forget.
If you fail today, succeed tomorrow.
If you've gambled and lost, learn and move on.
If you ever feel lost, turn to God

This Week's Hope Initiative:

Life can be simple, so why make it harder? Think about something you've handled less favorably in the past. How would you do things differently?

Your Hopes for this Week:

_____

_____

_____

_____

Week 7:

Send an Encouraging E-mail

The best way to cheer yourself up is to try to cheer somebody else up.

—Mark Twain

I remember the feeling of being uplifted after a friend forwarded an inspirational e-mail to me. Sometimes we need reminders, or a dose of hope, every chance we get to prevent us from being preoccupied with our problems. Let's remember to look at the beauty of life and not focus on the negativity.

We could all use a little infusion of encouragement to get the day started. When I forwarded that same e-mail to another friend, that individual replied to my e-mail saying she was going through a rough time, and it really uplifted her. We hadn't spoken face-to-face in a while since we live miles apart, and it was a nice way to keep in touch.

Without bombarding someone else's inbox with tons of Spam, why don't you drop some encouragement or a funny joke to a friend or associate once in a while—something that can really lift his or her spirit. Here is a sample I created:

From: Shadonna Richards

To: You @ yahoo.ca

Date: May 31, 2008 (Time 00:00 EST)

Subject: FW: Message from a Guardian Angel

Dear Overwhelmed,

Why are you letting silly little things
Get you down in this life?
Didn't you realize that life is a test?
With mini lessons that must be met

You need the lows to balance the highs,
Welcome to this thing called life
You're not here for a free, easy ride
But to grow from lessons that make it worthwhile

You've been placed here for a little taste of life,
Don't fret or despair, you're only there a short while
No matter what you're going through.
Know that your Maker can carry you through

Don't let someone else's weakness
Cause you undue distress
And if you mess up, don't feel burned.
You're really only there to learn
Until you go through trials like every angel up here has

You can't appreciate your worldly life
Or the blessings that you have
You can't be strong, if you always have life easy
You can't be insightful, if you only meet nice people

It's all part of the plan
To put your life in God's hands.
Your problem's just a little phase
In this long track of life

We were there before you entered
And we'll be cheering you at the finish line
Keep making the better choice
Listen to your inner voice

You've got us angels watching over you,
Making sure you make it through
In this world, you want to be great,
You've got to go through every "thing"
All the pleasures and all the pains.
All the losses and all the gains
So in the morning when you get up,
Don't let anything get you down

And no matter what life throws at you,
Don't you ever lose your ground
Always think and do your best
And let us take care of the rest.

Peace,
Your Guardian Angel Team

This Week's Hope Initiative:

List five people who could use an encouraging e-mail or message and send them a kind word, a boost of encouragement, an uplifting story or a funny joke. You can also use the e-mail I wrote above, as long as you credit the source. Additionally, you can visit www.wow4u.com for words of wisdom delivered to your mailbox or view the many inspirational quotes, stories and poems listed on their site. Alternatively, if you prefer to infuse laughter and wish to share a joke to brighten a day, try this website for clean humor, www.cleanjoke.com.

Your Hopes for this Week:

_____

_____

_____

_____

Week 8:

Build a Strong Positive Mental Attitude

A strong positive mental attitude will create
more miracles than any wonder drug.

—Patricia Neal

Doctors have often said that having a positive mentality and optimistic outlook on life has played a key factor in the speedy recovery of some of their patients. We've all got that inner-warrior within us to rise above and overcome any trauma in our lives. It usually follows on the wings of a strong positive mentality that you can overcome any adversity. It's a matter of tapping into that resource.

An inspiring example of that came from one of my readers who phoned me at the local newspaper to comment on a previous column I had written in 1995. There was something different about this reader. She had an unusual splash of enthusiasm. An exceptionally spiritual, optimistic presence. Intelligent. An amazing sense of humor. Insightful. I also noticed she had difficulty speaking on the phone. Her speech seemed to be impaired to a degree. But she had such an extraordinary story to tell about her volunteer work in the community I was compelled to later interview her for another story.

However, I was not prepared for what I later found out about her. Her name was Bonnie and she was no ordinary high-spirited volunteer. She was also a quadriplegic (paralyzed from the neck down as a teenager) by an impaired driver.

Locked into a special wheelchair that enabled her to make calls with the use of her chin movements on a device, she was not poor in optimism, but rich in endurance and spirit.

Bonnie did not sink into a bath of self-pity. Instead, she rose out of a depressing situation. She didn't know her story would inspire many and encourage others through her bravery. Paralyzed from the neck down, doctors didn't expect her to live. Miraculously, she did. She braved 20 major operations, including five brain surgeries.

Bonnie could have easily been discouraged. Instead, she retained her determined spirit.

She never complains, say friends close to her. She was happy when she finally learned how to eat and talk again— actions we all take for granted. Though she developed a rare neurological progressive disorder, she's fighting it with a positive spirit. She's always busy, volunteering her time in the community despite her medical condition.

Bonnie could have easily given up on life. Instead, she lives each moment with vibrancy. A fulfilling life.

The warrior-like woman said to me that she has forgiven the man responsible for her condition and has moved on. A crucial element of moving forward in life and staying mentally fit.

I hadn't met anyone like her before. Someone who spends the majority of her time thinking positively and keeping her spirits up. A rarity. Bonnie was told that her positive mentality had a key role in her survival.

That's the kind of strong-spirited inner happiness we all want. One that does not depend on what's around us but what's within us. One of the hardest things to do is to train our minds to always focus on good thoughts, even if our world around us is crumbling. Bonnie taught me an important lesson. Your life becomes influenced by whatever you choose to focus on.

This Week's Hope Initiative:

Bonnie's triumph is a perfect example that it is not your circumstances but your thoughts that determine the outcome. Remember, we always have a choice on how we react to situations. Is there someone in your life or someone you know of who has overcome great adversity? How can you be inspired by his or her example?

Your Hopes for this Week:

_____

_____

_____

_____

Week 9:

Visualize Your Dream Career
Then Work Towards It

Dare to dream, but even more importantly, dare to put action behind your dreams.

—Josh Hinds

I interviewed the first season Canadian Idol runner up Toya Alexis for a feature story titled "Canada's Talented Teenager" back in 1994 when she was only 13-years-old. She was known as Latoya Lesmond, and at that time, she had just taken home the crown of the third annual Miss Canadian Talented Teens International Competition. She was also about to represent Canada at the televised Hal Jackson's Talented Teens International Competition in Washington, D.C.

I felt at that time she would go far in life. She was only 13, yet poised, intelligent, multi-talented and goal-focused—she dreamed of going further in life and already had a roadmap of how she would get there. Blessed with a powerful voice that can easily be matched with Whitney Houston and Mariah Carey, Toya was no stranger to winning competitions. Her long list of awards included best vocalist award for the first annual Young, Gifted and Black Talent showcase.

She was also an active participant in her community and had involved herself with numerous activities including United Way fundraising, Multi-cultural week and Drug Awareness Day. The teenager told me her special interests included acting (she later appeared in films), dancing, reading and volleyball, but her career goal was to become a professional entertainer.

She visualized where she wanted to go in life and today she continues to live her dream.

One of the judges at the contest at the time said, "You can do anything you want to as long as you plan your route on how to get there."

Toya worked hard and used her God-given talents to reach new heights. The gifted singer/songwriter placed sixth runner up in Canadian Idol's first season (a controversial decision that had people commenting she should have won the contest with her powerhouse vocals). She used her experience to launch her career. She later released her debut album (she wrote 18 of the 20 songs) in August, 2005. Her album soared to platinum. From the beginning, Toya planned and worked hard using her skill, talent and dedication to achieve her dream. Today, she blesses many with her extraordinary talent.

This Week's Hope Initiative:

List three things you've always dreamed of doing. It could be writing your life story, raising children of your own, travelling the world, volunteering, taking singing lessons or acting, among other goals. If you've not pursued any of your dreams, ask yourself what's stopping you?

Your Hopes for this Week:

_____

_____

_____

_____

Week 10:

Understand That Money Isn't Everything

*Money is a terrible master,
but an excellent servant.*

—P.T. Barnum

If money isn't everything, then why is it that many of us strive to make more of it, drive the latest cars, buy name brand clothes and footwear and enjoy expensive gifts? Why is it we feel if someone is making more money, he or she is automatically more successful and happier than someone making less?

A former associate of mine dreamed of his condo on the lake and wanted to make more money to afford the mortgage on his new home, not to mention his BMW. So he, of course, took up a second job. His work schedule began at 7:00 a.m. with his first job until about 4:00 p.m., and he began his second job at 5:00 p.m. to midnight. He did this five days a week!

However, he realized he was defeating his purpose after suffering from periods of burnout and withdrawal symptoms from his social life. I asked him how it was that he wanted to earn more to enjoy a good life but the earning was preventing him from enjoying his good life.

I recall when I was head-hunted into another job by a larger corporation some years ago. I was encouraged to take the position because the job title was more prestigious and the pay was far greater than what I was making even though I had enjoyed what I was doing in the lower paying job. The new company boasted a higher salary, bonuses and flexibility. It was my first crack at marketing where I would finally get to use my creative skills on the job. But boy, was I sorry later. I burned brightly at first only to burn out later. I found myself working 16-hour days and seven days a week if you include the work I had to take home with me and, of course, you never get paid for overtime in marketing.

I was drained by the time I reached home. Too tired to enjoy my hobbies or do my writing. I developed the workaholic habit which allowed me to skip lunch and work through breaks.

My duties included administration, writing, editing, producing, designing, layout, clerical files, client files, producing reports and spreadsheets, travelling, catering for client meetings, typesetting correspondence, organizing major events—and this was only a small portion of my duties. I didn't have to be a mathematician to figure out the equation. The money clearly wasn't worth it.

I was cancelling personal engagements with friends and family because of work obligations outside of business hours. I knew then I would rather have less pay and more time to sleep at night and have a life outside of work.

* * *

Money isn't everything. As a reminder, I keep a copy of a poem by an anonymous poet that says it all:

> Money can buy a house, but it can't buy a home
> Money can buy a bed, but it can't buy sleep
> Money can buy a clock, but it can't buy time
> Money can buy food, but it can't buy an appetite
> Money can buy a position, but it can't buy respect
> Money can buy blood, but it can't buy life
> Money can buy sex, but it can't buy love
> Money isn't everything!

This Week's Hope Initiative:

Understand that money is not everything by reflecting on the above poem. One woman blogged about keeping this poem, that I had tagged on the end of this story I wrote for the Metro—Toronto edition in 2001, pinned up in her room to remind her everyday.

Your Hopes for this Week:

_____

_____

_____

_____

Week 11:

Be Resilient

*Be so strong, so that nothing can
disturb your peace of mind.*

—Christian D. Larsen

When we find ourselves catapulted into negative situations, the experience can knock our spirits into despair. Resilience is the ability to bounce back after getting knocked down in life. It is the ability to learn from, move on and improve after setbacks. This admirable trait is essential to taking control of your destiny. Rubin "Hurricane" Carter is the true embodiment of the power of the human spirit bouncing back from great adversity. I met the former US prizefighter, who came to the Ontario Science Centre in 2000 to give a lecture to a sold out crowd. I later commented on my experience in my weekly column for the local newspaper.

Here was a man, who was unable to speak until he was 18-years-old due to a severe speech disorder, now being paid to address sold out audiences. A miracle!

He believed in his abilities. He never gave up hope despite his condition.

Carter had a very realistic chance of becoming a world champion middleweight fighter, but in 1966, at the age of 29, when all was going so well, had his life flipped upside down after being falsely imprisoned for 20 years for a crime he "did not or could not commit." His story was recounted in books, a song by Bob Dylan and the movie titled "The Hurricane" starring Oscar-winner Denzel Washington.

He could have easily given up hope during those 20 years in prison, but he believed he would overcome this atrocity despite the evidence against him.

Mr. Carter could have very easily been bitter, but instead, he chose to fill his mind with a burning hope that justice would one day be served.

The American boxer could have been resentful, after all, he missed 20 years of his life and that of his children growing up, but he left no room in his heart for negativity.

He knew then that his dream of ever competing professionally was over. But he never lost his faith that one day he would be released from prison and have a place again in society.

Twenty years was a long time to wait for justice. He missed competing for the world championship belt—but ironically, 35 years after being convicted, it was awarded to him for winning an even greater battle.

Rubin Carter was 63 when I saw him and looking extremely well especially given his circumstances. He had a new purpose and role to fulfill in the world. He talked to the audience about being the executive director of the International Association in Defense of the Wrongly Convicted and how he had also addressed the United Nations about the cause. He used his adversity to reach out and help others. By serving on various boards, he continues his crusade to assist wrongfully convicted people.

He delivered a message of hope and inspiration to all of us sitting in the auditorium that day. His message was clear. Dare to succeed against the odds. Dare to rise above your adversity.

Never lose hope—no matter how long it takes! Believe in yourself even when you feel alone in your battles.

This Week's Hope Initiative:

No matter what difficult or discouraging situation you may find yourself in, focus on getting your mind out of the circumstance first. When you are determined to get out of negative happenings, your actions usually follow the path paved by your thoughts.

Your Hopes for this Week:

_____

_____

_____

_____

Week 12:

Do Your Part to Combat Workplace Gossip

Avoid all perverse talk; stay away
from corrupt speech.

—Proverbs 4:24

Let's face it, in the workplace, gossip is the only force that actually travels quicker than e-mail and the information is often far from accurate or kind.

Mind you, there are various degrees of gossip. From the malignant type designed to inflict a wound on some poor, innocent soul's reputation to the benign.

A while back, an acquaintance relayed a horror story to me (not worth repeating) of how he became the victim of cruel and unusual rumors that cost him his job. He wanted to know if this painful topic was important enough for me to address. Well, here is what I wrote in an article for the *Metro—Toronto Edition* in 2000 which garnered many responses from readers who could relate to being a victim of office gossip.

Hurtful gossip is a verbally transmitted disease that attacks your thoughts, ruins lives, cripples reputations and thrives on belief. Nothing is more annoying than when you or someone close to you becomes the target of loose lips and idle brains. But unfortunately it can happen.

The good news is that this virus can be contained!

First, you must listen to yourself. Do you often put others down behind their backs? If you hear information about another person, do you automatically assume it is true? Even if the subject of such falsehood is not there to defend himself? If someone wants to give you the lowdown on a colleague or acquaintance, do you listen attentively or do you tell them you're not interested and you have no time for small talk? As the saying goes: Bright people talk about ideas, ordinary people talk about things and small people talk about other people. It takes two to gossip, so by listening, you become just as lamentable as the gossiper. One thing I notice is that people who take pleasure in belittling others often have low self-esteem or have gross faults of their own, most that are far worse than the subject of their put downs. Perhaps it is a subconscious way to try to take attention off their own faults by focusing on others.

What most people fail to realize is that by putting others down, they often look deplorable, *not* their subjects… they're telling people what type of individual they are.

* * *

To get rid of this virus, some points to remember are:

1. If you gossip, you've proven you're not trustworthy. People will always wonder what you could be saying about them, and as a result, you'll make enemies without even knowing it. I personally like to keep a distance of say, 10,000 words from anyone I perceive as a blabber mouth.

2. Gossip is like judging someone without a fair trial. If the defense is not there to represent himself, then dismiss it as a mistrial. Imagine how you would feel in that person's position.

3. It can be harmful in ways you can't imagine. Wars have been started by rumors.

4. If you ever feel the urge to get on the phone and spread hurtful rumors, just dial 1-900-mind-your-own-business.

5. Keep in mind that words have a way of miraculously travelling back to the source. There's a saying to "keep your words soft and tender because tomorrow you may have to eat them."

This Week's Hope Initiative:

Live peaceably with others. Be kind to those whom you work with. Avoid spreading rumors which could come back to haunt you later. And as an added bonus: List five qualities you like about your coworkers. It could be a smile, the fact that they bring you coffee, they work hard or they are raising their children well. Sometimes when we look at similarities and find good traits in people (and we all have positive and negative traits), we tend to see things differently.

Your Hopes for this Week:

_____

_____

_____

_____

Week 13:

Create a Solid Plan for Your Dream

*Great things can happen to ordinary people if they
work hard and never give up.*

—Orel Hershiser

You need to know where you want to go in life before you get there. Having an idea of what you want and a solid plan on how to get there is not only beneficial but necessary. To illustrate my point, a perfect example of what can happen when you create a solid plan for your dream from a young age would be a student I had interviewed in 1995 for my column. You could describe her as 17 years of hard work, optimism and ambition. I spoke to the local teenager (who was a new immigrant at the time) by the name of Jennifer. She came to Canada from Sierra Leone, in West Africa with a dream to make a difference. The ambitious student became the owner of her own company, Little Elf, a multipurpose agency whose motto was "Extra hands for busy people."

She offered a wide range of services from typing and academic tutoring to planning kids' parties to care giving relief/babysitting and personal shopping for those who were unable to do it for themselves.

"It's difficult to find a full-time summer job," said the teen, "So I figured why not employ myself."

Jennifer was yet another example of hundreds of youths taking the initiative to create their own employment opportunities and provide services to the community. This would only be the beginning of her long-term goal to be a leader in the business world. At 17, Jennifer graduated as an Ontario Scholar and told me she planned to attend University of Toronto to study Business Administration and further her studies after that.

She especially loved reading business books, and with encouragement from her teachers, she embarked on her own research into the laws and regulations to open her own business. She was also a part of the YMCA Black Achievers program that helped her meet friends with similar interests.

Family support is invaluable to any child with a dream, and Jennifer knows that very well. She told me that her mother is her major supporter and she received great encouragement and guidance from her mom who would help deliver flyers for her business. She told me she enjoys helping senior citizens and parents with small children.

Today, Jennifer not only graduated from University of Toronto with Honors Management and Accounting with high distinction. She subsequently graduated from Harvard University Law School with her Juris Doctor degree in 2007. Today she is an associate lawyer at an international law firm in the U.S.

This Week's Hope Initiative:

If you have a dream, work hard and plan your way. Any place worth going is worth a carefully thought out plan. Gather resources, network and reach out to others. Any dream is possible. But most of all, never give up and never stop learning.

Your Hopes for this Week:

_____

_____

_____

_____

Week 14:

Take Better Care of Your Heart

Life is not merely to be alive, but to be well.

—Marcus Valerius Martial

Are you good to your heart? Ask yourself these questions: Do you try to do it all? Get angry easily? Find fault with everything? Neglect your diet? Set unrealistic goals? Bottle up your emotions? Get very little sleep or rest? Are you impatient? Do you neglect proper exercise or activity? Are you spending too much time online?

This last question may come as a surprise to some, but I was gripped by an article in *The New York Times*, from 2005, that featured the story about Lee, a 28-year-old South Korean man, who died after playing an online Internet game for 50 hours straight at an Internet café. According to those reports, Lee had neglected sleep, ate very little during that time and had apparently died from heart failure related to exhaustion. Coincidentally, prior to that, he had lost his job because he was spending too much time playing games on the computer.

The Internet can be fun and resourceful in gathering information, networking or conducting personal and professional business. I admit I spend a lot of time online doing research related to my writing, in addition to networking with my friends and overseas relatives, but like everything, moderation is a must. It's easy to get carried away and lose track of precious time. Don't let that happen to you.

Spending too much time online can not only ruin relationships but your health as well. Set a daily limit of say, three hours, and don't exceed it. Spend the rest of the time out of virtual reality and into actual reality.

If you find yourself spending an inordinate amount of time in front of the computer or engaging in other time-consuming activities, then it's a good time to re-evaluate your life and your health. Talk to your physician about it. You can also take a free, five-minute simple stress test from the Heart and Stroke Foundation at *www.heartandstroke.ca*. The site boasts heart healthy recipes online in addition to various other resources. February is widely canvassed as Heart Month in Canada by the Heart and Stroke Foundation (HSF). The HSF, in addition to raising funds for research and health promotion, actively educates the public as to the care of their heart and recommends measures to prevent strokes. Now is the time to re-evaluate our lifestyles. The five main causes of heart attacks and strokes are tobacco, poor nutrition, high blood pressure, lack of physical activity and of course, stress! So it's crucial to take measures to effectively manage our lifestyles.

This Week's Hope Initiative:

Eat a well balanced diet. Engage in regular physical exercise, be active, practice deep breathing, meditate (learn to be still), learn CPR (how to save the life of your loved ones if needed), talk, pamper yourself, get enough sleep, and police the amount of time you spend online. Limit your cyberspace activities and maintain balance in your life.

Your Hopes for this Week:

_____

_____

_____

_____

Week 15:

Count Your Blessings

God gave us a gift of 86,400 seconds today.
Have you used one to say thank you?

—William Arthur Ward

When we tackle current problems, we tend to forget that all situations, like life itself, are temporary. We forget that storms never last, they come to pass. We discount how much we have achieved through lessons learned in the past. How much further we are today because of growth which comes only through hardship. We don't take into account how we've beaten the odds before and flourished in the face of adversity.

We need to practice counting our blessings every day. This often means remembering them. A patient of mine told me he always took breathing for granted until he developed a rare condition that made it difficult for him to breathe without being hooked up to oxygen.

When we think of abilities or items we don't have, we should remind ourselves of what we *do* have to put things into perspective. Someone once said that we have more blessings in our lives than things going wrong for us. We just don't notice. It's true when life is happily gliding by, we don't take much notice. But we need to practice an attitude of gratitude as author Sarah Ban Breathnach once wrote. If we had to write down the stuff going wrong for us, it would probably take a page. For the stuff going right for us, it would definitely fill a book. It's important to adopt a silver-lining mentality in the midst of hardship. That type of mentality is often fuel to propel your mind out of a discouraging situation. We can all experience hope when we embrace gratitude for the events going right for us and focus on the blessings we have and where we are going in life.

I always try to focus on what I do have rather than what I don't have when situations appear gloom. For instance, I struggled financially through nursing school and had, on a couple of occasions, gone to bed on an empty stomach. I was living on my own at the time, and never mind buying groceries, finding money for rent for my apartment was a challenge. I used to joke that this was only temporary, and although my bank account and stomach were empty, at least my mind was full of knowledge. The college I attended was at the other end of the mega-city, and it took me almost two hours to commute. I used to rise at 5:00 a.m. when it was still dark outside, and leave my home to go the bus stop at 6:00 a.m. with my heavy knapsack of textbooks. I shivered waiting for the bus. Instead of dwelling on my long 2-hour commute, I decided to focus on the fact that I can get a lot of reading and homework done on the train and stay ahead of my class assignments. My first class began at 8:00 a.m., and by noon, I was in the library for a couple of hours studying, researching, revising, working on papers and studying materials for tests followed by more classes. At 4:30 p.m., I was at my on-campus part-time job. At 8:30 p.m., I waited for the evening bus. By 10:30 p.m., I arrived home. It was dark once again. I felt like I hadn't seen my home in days. Some of my classmates were going through similar or more challenging hardships. I kept focusing on the blessings that I had, such as the opportunity to study at a reputable college, freedom, health and life itself. This propelled me through the difficult times.

This Week's Hope Initiative:

Beginning today, make it a habit to count your blessings everyday. From being able to breathe, for life itself, your family, your children, your friends, your freedom, your ability to walk, to talk, to use your limbs, to think, to read. The list can no doubt be endless! What are you thankful for? Make a list and refer to it everyday. At the end of this book, I've created a personal hope journal, a book of blessings for you to place your thoughts and feelings about the greatness happening in your life. Take the time to reflect on everything going favorably in your life—from the simple to the divine.

Your Hopes for this Week:

_____

_____

_____

_____

Week 16:

Use Effective Strategies to Cope with Office Politics

Four things for success: work and pray, think and believe.

—Dr. Norman Vincent Peale

We all deal with it or see it everyday. We may lose friends or jobs over it, but we seldom talk about or call it by its name. Office politics!

At one point in our working lives, we've all no doubt worked with or near someone who just seems to get under our skin, rubs us the wrong way, raises our blood pressure and lowers our morale on the job simultaneously. Why is it then that no one talks openly about it or seeks support for it? The problem is that sometimes it's so subtle we feel it's only happening in our world. But the truth is, if you're going through it, chances are that hundreds more are having the same experience. If you don't know how to develop skills to effectively deal with the negativity of your coworkers, it will control you and have an adverse effect on your job performance.

A while back, I remember seeing my coworker (a top notch employee) over by the fax machine suspiciously looking both ways to make sure no one was approaching. Afraid of getting caught, she quickly and nervously fed a document into the feeder, punched in several digits and hit the start key. The secret document? Her resume.

I went up to her, careful not to startle her.

"Hi, Lee (not her real name), are you okay?" I asked sympathetically referring to her morning confrontation with another coworker.

"Yeah, I'm okay," she replied, covering her pain.

"I thought you loved your job. You do it so well," I commented, glancing at her resume.

"I do. I love the work. Just not the people around here."

"Oh, Lee, you can't leave because of the people. Besides, we're not all like that. Don't let them drive you out of a good job or out of your mind."

"They're always picking on me. I haven't done anything to them," she continued teary-eyed.

Lee eventually left the company but found her new job worse than the first and later regretted the move.

Lee later told me she had learned a few valuable lessons about work politics. Such as when things get heated up at work, that's not always the best time to leave. Think of it like a relationship. Would you jump out of a disastrous one and right into another in the same distraught frame of mind? It's important to not be a "job-rebounder." You're bound to come up against the same characters anywhere you go. Continually switching jobs is not always the answer. If you really want to leave, at least try to work out issues first with the person in question or the workplace. Depart on a good note, if it is possible.

Lee later settled into a job (after a string of unsuccessful job placements). She told me she decided to change the way she viewed workplace situations since the same characters seemed to pop up in most places. She spoke up for herself this time and worked hard, focused on her job at hand and was kind to everyone, whether or not they were kind to her. She viewed her job as a nine-to-five gig and had other fun activities outside of work to create balance.

This Week's Hope Initiative:

What coping mechanisms do you find useful in the workplace? Think about your options: Talking to the person with whom you have a conflict? Your supervisor? Positive thinking? Meditation? Keeping away from office gossip? It could be a number of other things you find useful. Work is a part of life. We need to find ways of creating a balance within ourselves and at work in order to survive.

Your Hopes for this Week:

_____

_____

_____

_____

Week 17:

Put Yourself in the Boss' Shoes

*If you have time to whine and complain
about something, then you have the time
to do something about it.*

—Anthony J. D'Angelo

Not everyone is happy with their boss or how things are run at their workplace. People whine, they complain and they vent their frustrations. Many take it personally. Mind you, there is a time to vent when change must occur, but you have to know the difference between changing what must be changed and leaving things as they are for the sake of keeping your job.

I once had a boss who was famous for his bully tactics and reducing even CEOs to tears. His motto was: "Never come to me with a problem, unless you've got a solution." Most of the workers at the firm had warned me about him ahead of time. "Watch out for Mr. You-know-who, he doesn't have a life, and he doesn't want you to have one either...." They told me, "When he pushes you around, don't sit back and take it quietly...make a lot of noise at head office. The squeaky wheel always gets the grease."

I recall a Friday afternoon, the second week in my new position, when he overheard me making plans to see a show right after work. Later, he handed me a mountain of handwritten material that had to be "typeset and edited by the end of the day." He gave it to me at 5:00 when I was ready to leave. How did I take it? Personally? Did I flare up and storm out of his office...telling him where the report should go? Did I dare defy his orders? Well, I didn't feel very good at the time. In fact, I initially believed it was intentional. But I was always raised that it's never what happens to you, it's how you react to it.

So, I calmly asked if I could see him in his office (to the surprise of my coworkers), and I spoke to him about the situation. It was then I was told that he too had to miss out on plans he had made with his family, and because he was under pressure from demanding clients to get it done, he had no choice. In fact, he explained to me that many people didn't take the time to sit down with him. He was not out to make anyone's life hell! He was trying to get the job done...to see everyone pulling his weight not pouting his lips. At that time I was glad I didn't take it personally. When you enter the workplace, you must remember to put your pride on the shelf, check your ego at the door, park your attitude outside and wear your "bully"-proof vest.

At a seminar I attended, based on the book *Don't Sweat the Small Stuff*, we were asked to put ourselves in our boss' shoes—an eye-opening experience. Your boss is simply fulfilling his role. If you were in his position (or his shoes), you would more than likely carry out the same initiatives. We all have our own roles to play in an organization. Everywhere you go you are destined to meet a variety of managerial types (kind of like a good cop—bad cop scenario). There's the control freak who whips everything into shape; the peacemaker who smoothes out the edges; the office angel; the office devil; and so on.

The average person spends 51 hours a week or 100,000 hours over a lifetime at work. If you're having trouble adapting to your work environment, you're in a lot of trouble. Someone once told me (as he modified Mahatma Ghandi's quote) "be the change you want to see in others." After all, being frustrated and carrying feelings of resentment will hurt you more than the institution. Remember that most supervisors began as ordinary wage earners at the bottom of the corporate ladder. And, to my former associate who always complained that the boss was there to drive everyone crazy, I told him that before he flared up again when he's not happy with a task, try a little shoe switching first and attempt to understand where the boss is coming from. It may not change the situation right away, but you'll feel better until better comes.

This Week's Hope Initiative:

Sometimes it's easy to like someone when we discover common or admirable traits. Think of five qualities you like about your boss. It could be a simple aspect such as her smile or that she's a hard worker, or even the fact that he or she hired you in the first place. Keep these in mind when you feel at a loss for good things to think about him or her.

Your Hopes for this Week:

_____

_____

_____

_____

Week 18:

Practice Daily Self-Love and Acceptance

Good habits are worth being fanatical about.

—John Irving

Most of us are aware of the benefits to our bodies when we exercise at least three times per week. We know we should exercise to keep fit and stay healthy. We have to eat right from all the food groups and eliminate junk food to keep our bodies in optimal shape. We might even do sit ups daily if we want to develop a six-pack stomach or walk daily to increase circulation. We do these exercises not just once, but daily and regularly. So then why is it that when it comes to our most important asset and most fragile that we overlook the daily regime?

What do we need to do to shield ourselves from getting emotionally beat up, depressed, obsessed and stressed? This answer has come in many self-help books and daily meditation programs. We might even pick up an inspirational book once in a while to help us feel good about ourselves. Kudos to those who read the scriptures daily.

I know when I meditate and focus on positive thoughts it helps me through the day. We do need to be reminded of balance and self-love daily, every chance we get, because our egos, our emotions and our feelings take a hard lashing every day whether we realize it or not. We're always up against those who are not worthy of our emotions or feelings. I find the best time to do this is early in the morning or as I ride the train to work.

* * *

Create your own list of favorite quotes and rehearse them until they are ingrained in your mind. Pull them out as a shield of defense, strength or inspiration. Here are a few of my favorites:

- You are the most important person in your life; if you don't respect yourself, who will? (Author Unknown)

- The tests of life are not to break you but to make you. (Author Unknown)

- A man's life is what his thoughts make of it. (Marcus Aurelius)

- What other people think about you is none of your business. (Author Unknown)

- Fret not thyself over evil doers. (Psalm 37:1)

- Count your blessings every day. (Author Unknown)

- For every problem there is a solution. (Dr. Norman Vincent Peale—The Power of Positive Thinking)

- This is the day which the Lord has made; let us rejoice and be glad in it. (Psalm 118:24)

- I can do all things through Christ which strengthens me. (Philippians 4:13)

- He shall give his angels charge over thee. (Psalm 91:11)

- No weapon that is formed against thee shall prosper and every tongue that shall rise against thee in judgment, thou shall condemn. (Isaiah 54:17)

- All things work together for good to them that love God, to those who are called according to His purpose. (Romans 8:28)

- I have not seen the righteous forsaken. (Psalm 37:25)

This Week's Hope Initiative:

Make a list of some of your favorite quotes and mantras, then keep them posted for motivation and reminders to embrace your inner-beauty everyday.

Your Hopes for this Week:

_____

_____

_____

_____

Week 19:

Give the Gift of Love at Christmas Time

*Too often we underestimate the power
of a touch, a smile, a kind word, a listening
ear, an honest compliment or the smallest act
of caring, all of which have the potential to
turn a life around.*

—Leo Buscaglia

The spirit of Christmas has been diluted over the years with corporate marketing schemes and images of busy mall patrons preoccupied with showing their love in dollars and cents to family members and friends.

To some, Christmas means a holiday shopping spree, glittering Christmas trees and battered and abused credit cards. And for those who don't have family it could mean depression or loneliness. Christmas is about giving, not just dollars and material items, but most importantly love.

True love. Not a mask you pull out of your closet for Christmas day only to be discarded with the leftover turkey bones. Love unites all the positive human emotions that we all experience, to share with those we care about. Love shouldn't be measured by outstanding credit card debt. And writing a check doesn't mean you have sufficient funds in the emotional bank of love. It's not a passive thought or an inactive verb, but love is an active emotion providing warmth, comfort, understanding and respect to the receiver. The greatest present is within you. The greatest present is to unwrap the gift of true divine love, opening the fountain of ever flowing happiness from your soul to everyone. Your very being, body, mind and soul encompasses a gift that is irreplaceable and invaluable to the receiver.

SMILE: Dolly Parton once said if you see someone without a smile, give them yours. A smile costs nothing but gives so much to the receiver, and according to some experts, it can improve the looks of the giver.

WORDS: Offer words of inspiration or encouragement whenever you can. For instance, if you see your friend or loved one looking especially nice one day, or being his or her usual charming self, say so. Often people take the time to complain when things go wrong, but they rarely take the time to mention when everything is going right. People who do good deeds can often be compared to housework, which is never noticed unless it's not done.

A helping HAND is always an arm's length away, it has been said. When extended to the poor and the needy it could mean a world of difference and shows you really care.

Because the holidays can be so lonely for some and depression is often magnified, merely being there for someone and showing him love and affection is saying a lot. When your loved one asks you for your help, instead of offering a cold shoulder, why not provide a warm shoulder to lean on. We could all use a shoulder to cry on or to lean on in times of despair or confusion. We all need friends and people to talk to and to stand by us. For me, the greatest Christmas gift is the gift of life. Having a wonderful family, close friends and acquaintances I will cherish to the end of time.

This Week's Hope Initiative:

Make a special Christmas List (or a list for whichever holiday you celebrate) to give a gift from the heart to those you care deeply about.

1. _____
2. _____
3. _____
4. _____
5. _____
6. _____
7. _____
8. _____
9. _____
10. _____
11. _____
12. _____

Your Hopes for this Week:

_____

_____

_____

_____

Week 20:

Know When to Walk Away from a Fight

It is an honor for a man to stay out of a fight.
Only fools insist on quarrelling.

—Proverbs 24:23

Forget about your ego for a moment in a confrontation. Undoubtedly, we've all been in a situation where we are opposite a person we deem annoying or who is so argumentative in nature that he'd pick a fight with a lamp post if it got in his way. Well, I've been there. The subject was a used car salesman I visited a while back. He had a temper that erupted like a volcano.

The problem was I had asked him too many questions, and he flared up to the point where he didn't want to back down. The trouble was he didn't want to show me documents pertaining to the car, like its buyer history, which is mandatory in the province of Ontario.

So what would any sane person do? Walk away, right? Would you believe that not everyone who has met him has? Of course, if someone hurls insults and put downs at you, the way he did, you may be tempted to challenge him. This, of course, would make things worse. Tempted as I was to put him in his place, I quietly ignored his behavior and decided to walk away politely stating I was no longer interested. To my surprise, he continued to argue as I walked away. My grandmother always used to say that it takes courage and self-control to be able to walk away from a fight. Strive to keep the peace in a confrontation.

This Week's Hope Initiative:

Some tips to remember in a civil argument: Remain calm and levelheaded; avoid hurling insults; deal with the issue at hand; listen to the other person; talk it out with mutual respect.

Your Hopes for this Week:

_____

_____

_____

_____

Week 21:

Make Every Moment Count

When the one you love is taken away
Seems like nothing can detract the pain
Our only hope is to keep them alive
By remembering all the good times

Honoring their past life
And how they've touched our life
We know they must move on
Their work here has been done

Back into the hands of God
Where they can now watch over us
Memories keep loved ones alive
It's memories of them that will never die.

There's no easy way to accept the loss of a loved one. Knowing that you'll never see or talk to them again is one of the hardest pains to endure. But it has been said that over time it can make us strong.

Sadly, when one of my younger brothers died at the age of 19, I was beyond devastated. For the first time, I felt like part of my world collapsed before me. I was numb with shock and began a rampant questioning period with sentences beginning with "Why?" and "How?" He was so brilliant and talented. He had so much ahead of him for which to live. We tend to believe that is sufficient enough to guarantee a future of 50 to 75 more years on this earth. Up until that point, I used to avoid the "D" word like the plague. But as my pastor once said, "Death is not the end of life but a part of life." We all seem to live each day believing that our family and close friends are always going to be around.

The death of someone close to us forces us to re-examine our lives and open our eyes to see things that we didn't recognize before. We must value life and treasure each breath we take. We must value each person and how he or she touches our lives everyday. When I was asked to write his eulogy, I knew it would be the most difficult prose I would pen. Rodney was so young and was, after all, still my baby brother. I was forced to say goodbye and review his short but full life. One of the last sentiments I said to Rodney on one of our Big Sis/Little Brother talks was that he should think about his future and what he was going to do with the rest of his life. Thinking back now, I would have said, "Rod, we don't know how long we have to live; the future depends on our present. Live fully in the moment and make the most of every second you have." I used to take it for granted he would always be around and one day grow up to get married, be saddled with a mortgage, and play football with his grandchildren. After his sudden death, I know I'll never take anything in life for granted again.

* * *

Through the death of a loved, remember this:

1. We must celebrate the life they've lived. Remember all the good times.

2. No one can take away the happy memories, as I was kindly reminded by my former boss, Barry.

3. We are not here forever. We must all realize we have a limited time. We could be here for a hundred years or less. So we must make the most of each second we have, enjoy life in the present and spend as much time with the ones we love.

4. Create as many happy moments with your loved ones, because soon they become memories and when they are gone from us, memories are what live on forever.

This Week's Hope Initiative:

*Think of the happiest moments you have spent with those
close to you. What were they? Make a list and always
cherish them. In fact, aim to create more enjoyable moments
with those you love.*

Your Hopes for this Week:

_____

_____

_____

_____

Week 22:

Put Things into Perspective

If you don't like something, change the way you think about it. Don't complain.

—Dr. Maya Angelou

For a nation that has so much, we sure complain a lot. We complain of car insurance rate hikes, fare increases, cell phone rates, being ripped off by the long distance companies, and crashing computers among other things. These are all valid gripes, mind you, but I was having a conversation with a friend who put things into perspective. Think of what it would be like if we didn't have the items or technologies we are complaining about now.

I admit, sometimes when I'm on the computer and it shuts down in the middle of an essay, I curse. It freezes. I wait. It recovers. My text is lost, and so I have to retype what I've lost and remember to save it every five seconds in case it happens again. But it wasn't long ago we were using typewriters which cannot compare to the ease and luxury of working with computers. Saving files on disks, correcting and adding text without having to re-type an entire document, especially if it's 200 pages long, is a blessing. Compared to the typewriter, my technical problems with the computer didn't look so bad after all.

I recently read an article that said it all. Like many writers today, I have luxuries, where writing equipment is concerned, that Shakespeare could never have dreamed of. A teenager today with his cell phone, computer games, iPod, television, stereo and home entertainment systems is living a life of luxury that a King of England 500 years ago could not even begin to imagine.

Even today, we are living like royalty compared to the poor in underdeveloped countries. We have such conveniences, we don't even realize how grateful we should be. Sure, when we are introduced to new technology we're going to have teething problems that hurt, but it beats having to chew with our gums.

This Week's Hope Initiative:

Try to think of five gadgets you have working in your life, that weren't around 20 or even 30 years ago. How would you live without them in this modern age?

Your Hopes for this Week:

_____

_____

_____

_____

Week 23:

Set a Good Example in Life

Setting an example is the best sermon.
—English Proverb

Sometimes the way we live and the example we set have a profound effect on others.

I was one of the millions of people who descended upon the gates of Kensington Palace in England's capital in September 1997 to pay my respects to the late Princess of Wales.

The tragic death of Diana, Princess of Wales, hadn't hit me until I actually went up to her Kensington Palace home on the day before her funeral, a few short hours before her body arrived in the hearse for her last night in London. At that time, I was living and working in London at the *British Medical Journal.*

As if it were a member of my own family, I had cancelled personal plans for the weekend, and along with my colleagues, changed my work schedule to prepare for the day of mourning on Saturday, September 6. What was it about this beautiful, kind-hearted princess that touched so many? She was a Godsend and had blessed so many people by her selfless good deeds. That is why her sudden death shocked so many, including myself.

It simply didn't seem real or fair. Diana truly represented all that was good in humanity in all of us. She reached out to the poor, the rejected, the lonely, and the sick. She had a natural gift of making people feel special even when society shunned them. Let's not forget the time she held the hand of an AIDS patient back in the 1980s, at a time when there was negative public perception about the disease.

79

At that time, people had misconceptions of catching it through hand contact.

When I had left work early on Friday to go to Kensington Palace, the crowded tube (London's underground train system) was filled with students, business people and other ordinary people, most with cards and fresh flowers in their hands. I didn't have to ask directions—even though it was my first time to the palace. My colleague, Lorraine, and I followed the people walking with bouquets in their hands, all headed towards a common destination.

It was raining that Friday as I laid my carnations at the gate of the palace among the millions already placed. Only then did Diana's death begin to slowly sink in.

I've never experienced anything quite like it before. I've never before seen so many floral arrangements. It was a sea of petals, and the aroma of scented candles permeated the air. I was among hundreds of thousands of people, yet if I closed my eyes, I would think that I was alone, because the crowd was so quiet, solemn, and respectful.

People from all over the world came to pay their respects. I can recall an elderly man squeezing my shoulder and shaking his head as he placed his own flowers at the gate beside mine. It was as if we were part of the same family. People patted shoulders of strangers. Teary eyed. Dazed.

This was the effect Diana had on humanity, on our hearts. I remember on the Saturday that shops, cinemas, and most businesses were closed as a mark of respect. Supermarket parking lots were deserted as if no one lived in the city. On the day of the funeral, an estimated two million people lined the streets of London. Most camped out the night before.

We were sad because Diana reminded us of ourselves with her vulnerabilities and her down-to-earth, graceful manner. A colleague of mine told me he'd "never felt so hurt over someone he never met." I felt the same way.

I read the other messages written while I glanced at the flowers: "I will never again take life for granted." "You are the princess of our hearts...forever." And, "These flowers may die soon, but you are a beautiful rose that will live on forever in our hearts." Her funeral was televised live to almost 2.5 billion viewers around the world. Diana left behind her two young sons, Prince William and Prince Harry. She had countless charitable commitments, especially her involvement with the Red Cross.

The lessons Princess Diana brought to this world were that:

1. People will always remember you for how you treat them—spiritually speaking, and

2. It's not the years in your life but the life in your years that count, as the saying echoes.

She had blessed so many and because of that her legacy lives on. Princess Diana injected a magical flow of love into the world's social stream, to heal those who were hurting, the lonely, the oppressed, the people of the world, and she will live forever in our hearts.

This Week's Hope Initiative:

How can you be a blessing to others? Look for ways to give back and to be kind without expecting anything in return.

Your Hopes for this Week:

_____

_____

_____

_____

Week 24:

Learn the Secrets to Living Well from a 105-year-old

*Learn from yesterday, live for today,
and hope for tomorrow.*

—Albert Einstein

What do you think people will say about you after you're gone? That you lived a life worthwhile? You were devoted to your family? You were an inspiration and a role model to your friends and loved ones? You were always there for others when they needed your help?

When I gave my great-grandmother's eulogy in 1994, it wasn't hard to come up with great praise for her. Her name was Estina Mirina Whitter. She passed away in her sleep at age 105 years, and she was very much loved. She gave love in abundance. Though she suffered a lot during her young days, she never ceased to be optimistic about the future. After her funeral service, everyone walked away with a feeling of gratitude that they had known her. She left a legacy of hope behind. She found her own medicine to cope with life for each of the 38,325 days she'd lived. Her youthful skin breathed a century of experience, wisdom, heartache and joy. The Bible and all of its messages were her sole source of inspiration and motivation and shaped the way she lived. She exemplified courage and honor. She followed many simple rules including:

FORGIVENESS: The Bible says: "Blessed are the merciful, for they shall obtain mercy."

I remember when we sat down together before her death, and she shed a tear in remembrance of Bauder, her son who died many decades ago at the age of 18. His life was brutally cut short by a jealous rival. But everyone remembers the story of how the murderer, who served five years, came out looking for her and begging forgiveness which she gave with open arms. Many wondered how she could forgive him after what he had done. She replied, "Who am I not to forgive? Jesus forgives us all the time." Perhaps the faith providing her strength and comfort kept her heart beating those 105 years.

COURAGE WITHOUT WORRY: A scripture reads: "A cheerful heart is good medicine. But a broken spirit dries up the bone."

Estina would seldom worry. It baffles many to this day how she reacted to the news from her doctor that she was diagnosed cancer during her late 70s. The doctor told her she didn't have much longer to live. She took the news very well as if nothing was wrong. She continued to live her life in abundance and focused on making the most of her moments. Later, with treatment, the disease went into remission. She kept her spirits up despite the news and continued to live well. In fact, she not only outlived the disease but had no other health problems. She lived much longer than anyone could have imagined. She was a true survivor. She defied the odds. Defied time. Defied her age. Her skin never wrinkled under the pressures of time. Her energy and wisdom only increased. Many wondered how she did it.

KINDNESS: Estina was kind. Exceptionally kind. She did not have much in material assets, but made up for it ten-fold spiritually. She was a nurse midwife who safely delivered hundreds of babies for poor villagers for little or no pay, at all hours. Sometimes awakened in the middle of the night, she would travel through the countryside on her mission.

Another legacy of hope she left behind was her story of looking for the good in others. She would tell her children, if someone does you 99 wrongs and one good, you remember the good they have done for you. Forgive. Eliminate worry, negativity and doubt from your mind.

Laugh a lot. Pray a lot. Work hard. Be honest. Have good intentions. Share. Care. Always be there, for one another. It is not your material possessions but your legacy of kindness, love and charity that you leave behind in this world for which you'll best be remembered.

FAITH: She was a God-fearing, God-loving woman of hope who cared for the emotional and physical needs of not just her own children but others in her village.

FAMILY: To her children, she was hope and love. To her grandchildren, she was wisdom and courage. To her great-grandchildren, she was a walking, talking history book. To her great-great-grandchildren, she was a legend, unknown to the rest of the world. To those who knew her during her 105 years on earth, she was a woman who may have been low on assets but high in compassion. She was perhaps viewed as poor in society, but she was genuinely rich in good deeds. Her life sang of hope and joy despite pain and suffering. She was a living, human instrument who sang of hope. She was an embodiment of peace. A pillar of courage. She exemplified inner strength and beauty. She was willing, able and ready for anything life would bestow on her.

I am so proud to have known Ms. Estina Whitter and to have the wonderful fortune to call her my great-grandmother.

This Week's Hope Initiative:

What spiritual legacy are you leaving behind for those close to you? Will you be remembered for your kindness? Your laughter? The joy or helping hand you've given to others? It's not too late to start one now. Live and share your legacy of love today.

Your Hopes for this Week:

_____

_____

_____

_____

Week 25:

Create Your Own Path

If you plant perseverance, you will reap victory.

—Brian Tracy

Successful achievers don't necessarily follow a path, they make one. A powerful example of that was expressed in the *Scarborough Mirror* column I wrote in 1995 on a superstar NHL player. In 1981 when six-year-old Kevin Weekes began playing hockey in the city, the National Hockey League still didn't have its first black goalie. Today, Weekes plays for the New Jersey Devils with an impressive record behind him. When I visited the then 20-year-old Toronto-born NHL player at his home for an interview, he was playing for the Florida Panthers. He later was recruited for other teams including the New York Rangers. He was at that time one of the few black, Canadian NHL goalies.

Upon meeting Weekes, one notices the obvious. That he speaks like an Ivy League graduate, so calm, sophisticated and intelligent and confident, way beyond his years. With a history of determination, hard work, strong family values and immeasurable support from his parents, it's not surprising that Weekes is where he is today.

He began playing hockey at age six for St. Michael's in Toronto and was the youngest to play for the Toronto Red Wings beginning at the age of eight for nine consecutive seasons. He was drafted by the Ontario Hockey League in 1992.

Weekes was "ranked the second goalie in the world for the NHL draft in 1993." He was selected by the Panthers as their second pick, attending their training camp and subsequently signed a three-year contract.

Since there are very few black players in the NHL, Weekes added that "hopefully this can motivate" younger kids that no matter what background you're from, you can accomplish your dreams and achieve your goals (no pun intended).

As if spending a considerable amount of time practicing, working out at the gym, reading and attending meetings doesn't keep him busy enough, the young goalie always makes time to volunteer and work with younger children.

At the time, Weekes was also involved in the innovative Alternative Sports organization that has, among other amenities, a hockey camp. "The focus is to encourage young ethnic kids to participate and compete in hockey," Weekes said in that interview.

It's unquestionable that Weeks is not only physically fit but mentally fit. He strongly believes one's mind is his or her greatest asset. He added that sometimes your body may seem tired and unable to finish a task, but if your mindset is on go, it can easily override your body's decision to call it quits.

Yes, it's true! You'd be surprised at how much you can do when you put your mind to it.

This Week's Hope Initiative:

Create your own path. If you want to reach a destination but you don't see any clear marked way of getting there or footsteps to follow, then start making foot prints in the sands of life.

Your Hopes for this Week:

_____

_____

_____

_____

Week 26:

Appreciate the True Value of Your Parents

A mother's love is a gift from above.

—Author Unknown

"Being mom isn't an easy job, but at least you have job security, seven days a week for life!"

The above quote began my humorous Mother's Day column for the local newspaper in 1995. That was the inscription on a Mother's Day mug that my younger sister pointed out to me while we were shopping for that special gift at a department store. Yes, it was Mother's Day. And I reflected on the 17 hours of labor that Mom had endured and so many years later. I am still grateful for the irreplaceable gift of life that was given to me by my mother.

Using my grandmother and mother as examples, I decided to do a breakdown of the most respectable yet underpaid job in the world.

Job title: Mother.

Description: Our mothers play not just one role, but 100 different positions in our lives, if you stop and think about it. I wrote a mock fee-breakdown for that time period to take a look at a few of her jobs and what it would be worth on the market (per hour) had Mom been paid to do them. Caregiver $12, cook $15, teacher $16, chauffer, $30, spiritual advisor $20, maid $9, waitress $8 plus tips, fashion consultant $30, doctor-whatever OHIP pays, nurse $30, and therapist $60. This does not include those invaluable capacities such as being a best friend and confidante, and comedian when you're feeling down. This works out to be at least $200 an hour. Multiplied by 24 hours on-call comes up to an astonishing $4,800 a day! That's $33,600 a week,

$134,000 a month or $1.6 million a year! Before taxes, of course.

So in short, we really couldn't afford to have a mother (or father) if the wages came out of our pockets. Of course, you can't put a price tag on being a mother and you wouldn't want to. But it's nice to know we can always appreciate and value Mom all year around.

This Week's Hope Initiative:

When you are thinking of what gift to give to your mother on Mother's Day or Dad on Father's Day, think of all the wonderful roles she or he has played in your life. Better yet, why wait until a designated day to show your appreciation? Why not honor your parents every day?

Your Hopes for this Week:

_____

_____

_____

_____

Week 27:

Take Advice on Love from Golden Couples

The best and most beautiful things in the world cannot be seen or even touched. They must be felt with the heart.

—Helen Keller

Some say they don't believe in love at first sight, but I have proof it does happen and the results can be magical.

At 17, my grandmother, Nesitta, met my grandfather, Godwin, who was 21. They fell in love at first sight and have been happily married ever since. They are just as close now as they were back then. Much like fine wine, their love and devotion for each other has only flourished with time. Their secret? Being a curious writer, I had to sit down and pick their brains for some answers as to how they did it with divorce rates in our day so outstandingly high. The secret is—there is no secret, only sophisticated common sense.

* * *

Lessons on love from this Golden Couple:

1. They love each other with their hearts and their minds. It has been said that to love with the heart is adoration but to love with the mind is admiration. They adore, admire and respect each other.

2. They are each other's best friend. They can talk openly and honestly with each other about anything and everything. They've built a solid foundation on friendship.

3. They understand each other. They listen to each other's concerns, fears and aspirations.

4. They understand that love is about growth.

5. They add humor and optimism to their spiritual diet. They enjoy similar interests and spend time laughing and talking together.

6. Trust is critical. They can be open and truthful about everything.

7. Acceptance. They are non-judgmental with each other. Love means "in spite of" because no one is perfect. Love means truly loving a person in spite of his faults. Love is a powerful emotion that unites all the positive human emotions. It's the most valuable gift you can give another human being, yet it costs very little, if anything.

This Week's Hope Initiative:

What lessons can you learn from a golden couple who have been married for at least half a century? How will you apply them to your own relationship?

Your Hopes for this Week:

_____

_____

_____

_____

Never Underestimate the Power of a Miracle

In all things, it is better to hope than to despair.

—Goethe

It has been said that a misty morning does not necessarily signify a cloudy day. In other words, you may not see it now but things have a way of clearing themselves up.

Further proof of that comes from the story of Daniel Burton whom I wrote about for the *Rouge Valley Mirror*. He was a nine-year-old Pickering boy with leukemia, who had to fight odds of 1 in 750,000 to find a matching bone marrow donor. His father had ruled out finding the right donor for his son comparing it to the odds of winning the lottery.

Despite staggering odds, a matching donor was found within weeks! Just when they felt they had exhausted all resources.

It's times such as these we believe that in the face of adversity there is hope. Situations can get better, no matter how discouraging they seem. It could be an illness, an accident or a failure in your life.

Nothing is impossible!

Of course, there are high points that often help us along our rocky road to recovery such as family support. Nothing beats spiritual support, unconditional love and the closeness of people there for us in sickness and in health. This goes for supportive friends who are there to cheer you up and lift your spirits. Friends who are there for you in your time of need, not just on your problem-free days. Research is also important. It's good to know about resources in your community and to learn about the types of programs available to persons who are in similar situations like yourself.

And finally, nothing beats a winning attitude. It's not about what happens to us but our reaction to it that matters. Doctors have often said that attitude played an important part in the recovery of some of their patients.

This Week's Hope Initiative:

If you know someone who is in a situation similar to Daniel, you may want to check out the website for the Gift of Hope Organ and Tissue Donor information in the U.S. at www.giftofhope.org. (Not related to this book). Or in Canada, the Trillium Gift of Life Network at www.giftoflife.on.ca.

Your Hopes for this Week:

_____

_____

_____

_____

Week 29:

Focus on Your Strengths Not Your Weakness

Happiness comes from within, not without.

—David Denotaris

Yes, it helps to have a positive outlook on life. No matter what happens. You have to be strong or at least be a person who can adapt to change and move on. In 1995, I interviewed Gary for my column. His outlook on life was incredible considering what he'd been through.

Gary's jolly spirit was contagious as he spoke with energy and excitement. The former construction worker's greatest test was to rebuild his own life after being stricken with Multiple Sclerosis in 1974.

Years later, he braved many operations in his next battle. Cancer. Unable to move from his neck down, his condition worsened, but not his mindset. Don't tell Gary what he can't do.

He looks at what he can *still* do, not what he can no longer do. Instead of sinking into self-pity, he shifted his attention to working in the community helping others like himself to cope with their situations. With his expertise in construction, he's able to offer advice on constructing buildings for people with special needs.

Gary could have easily given in to his situation and dwelt on his loss of certain abilities, but to live a life of spiritual well-being, he chose to focus on what he is still capable of doing and found strength in his ability to reach out to others in a positive way.

He also offers insight and advice to others on how to cope with their disability. "So I've been dealt a rotten hand (in life)," he told me during that phone interview with a hearty laugh. "The important thing is, I'm playing it well."

This Week's Hope Initiative:

Some of the happiest people in the world are not happy because they have everything but because they make the best of what they do have! Some of the happiest people in the world aren't happy because things are going perfectly for them but because they handle themselves perfectly even when their world is not perfect. What can you do differently in your imperfect world?

Your Hopes for this Week:

_____

_____

_____

_____

Week 30:

Remember the Angels in Your Life

A wise man remembers his friends at all times;
a fool, only when he has need of them.

—Turkish Proverb

I wrote the following poem that was published in the *Toronto Sun* in 2000 under the title People.

There'll be people who let you down,
Don't appreciate you,
talk behind your back,
Torment you, test you
and ultimately lose your trust

And for every one,

There'll be people,
who sincerely appreciate you,
Encourage you, believe in you,
Care about you, are there for you,

Praise you behind your back,
Love you unconditionally,
And always lift you up.
When you're up against those who are unkind
Remember the angels in your life
Who have been by your side.

This Week's Hope Initiative:

Who are the earth angels in your life? Write a list and make it a point to tell each one how much you appreciate his or her friendship or his or her relationship. There's no better time than the present. When you feel discouraged by others, remember there are always people in your life who love you and care about you whether you realize it or not.

Your Hopes for this Week:

_____

_____

_____

_____

Don't Be Too Hard on Yourself When Searching for Love

In the middle of difficulty lies opportunity.

—Albert Einstein

"Is there anything wrong with me?" a friend once asked me.

"No, why?" I queried with a puzzled expression.

"Then, why am I alone?"

Some call it the ultimate question with the elusive answer. I told him that chemistry and connecting is not a science that produces exact results if you follow the right procedure. Sometimes it's about opportunity.

I know too many wonderful people who can't seem to connect with Mr. or Miss Right. Sometimes it's about being in the right place at the right time! I told my friend not to be too hard on himself. Not everyone connects right away. It's not like going to school, honing skills and applying for a job or going to the store with enough money to buy a product.

You can't just go into a mall and announce, "I'm going to get me a Mr. Right or Miss Right!" This is not a caveman's world where you simply bang someone over the head and drag her to your cave and she is yours forever. You may love someone who doesn't feel the same or vice versa.

What are you to do? If it were that easy, everyone who wants to be in a relationship would be in a relationship. It's important to be yourself and treasure those around you who love you. Don't stop looking for love. Just don't stop living either. A former associate of mine told me she was taking a break from actively looking for love and instead re-channeled her energy to focus on her volunteer work and meeting and helping others. She later met her future husband that way.

This Week's Hope Initiative:

What other areas in your life could use some attention? Try joining a few good organizations in your locale such as the local gym, community group, sports club, or church. Enrich your life.

Your Hopes for this Week:

_____

_____

_____

_____

Week 32:

Clarify, Don't Crucify

Faults are thick where love is thin.

—Danish Proverb

We've all been in a situation where we've heard something less than flattering about ourselves from someone.

What is our first instinct? Challenge it and say, how dare they? Who do they think they are? Do we ever take the time to actually confront that individual? Rarely.

It has been said that one in four friendships end in misunderstanding, misspoken words or miscommunication. I was in a situation where I heard something that didn't seem quite right, the bearer of the bad news told me to never talk to that person again, but I had to clarify first before I took that step. After confronting the individual, I learned the statement was totally taken out of context. I was satisfied with the results, and I let it go. I could have lost a valuable work relationship had I merely accused or misjudged a person based on hearsay. I always believe in giving people what I would want for myself. The BOD (benefit of doubt).

I assume the best, until proven otherwise. And hearsay is not valid proof.

This Week's Hope Initiative:

Are there any holes in your relationships that could use some filling? Any outstanding misunderstandings? Try clarifying miscommunications as you learn and grow.

Your Hopes for this Week:

_____

_____

_____

_____

Week 33:

Forget about Your Age

It matters not how long we live, but how we live.

—Author Unknown

It's true that you're as old as you feel and your age is just a number. Nothing could ring more true for one of the cheeriest volunteers I interviewed for the local newspaper in 1994. She was driven by the desire to help others. I spoke to Joanne, one of the city's most active volunteers, a slender, physically fit, 82-year-old model, after she became the recipient of the Ontario Senior Achievement Award.

The local fashion model explained to me, "I've been busy all my life. Being busy keeps me alive, it keeps me hopping and it keeps me out of mischief." The golden girl laughed at her confession.

An enthusiastic great-grandmother, Joanne was personally congratulated by the Premier, Lieutenant Governor and Minister of Citizenship at the time. Her remarkable contributions to the community stemmed from her years of hard work and dedication. Since the Second World War, she had been busy, non-stop, dedicating much of her time to volunteer work in the community.

Joanne delivered communion to the sick, provided community service to the disadvantaged and she actively engaged in fundraising projects for the needy. Doing more than what most people half her age do, she was also the public relations coordinator for a local bowling club. She was awarded a gold pin by the Government of Ontario for more than 15 years of extraordinary service and her contributions as a volunteer. "It's the story of my life," she told me, "I'm always busy doing something, and I love it!"

It was almost a challenge keeping up with the 82-year-old, high-spirited resident who kept herself busy whether it was baking goods for the needy, coordinating fundraising events and social activities for senior citizens or posing as a runway model for her association's Ladies Auxiliary annual fall fashion show. Joanne firmly believed you're never too old to do anything. At the time, she had two children, six grandchildren and one great-grandson. She still enjoyed playing bridge with her "girlfriends." And after 47 years of driving, she still loved getting behind the wheel of her car.

Born on November 4, 1912, the year the Titanic sank, Joanne knew that the secret to living life to the fullest was maintaining a healthy spiritual diet of optimism, enthusiasm and bucket loads of humor.

Years later, I also had the privilege of doing one of my nursing community placements at a walk-in clinic. It was an eye-opening experience. Once again, I learned that age is nothing but a number.

I couldn't help but notice a couple who came in giggling. They looked as if they had just finished working out or walking, dressed in their adorable matching jogging suits. They were having a ball. He gave her a surreptitious pinch from behind, and she jolted up and giggled again. It looked as if they couldn't keep their hands off each other. I thought it was so cute. They hadn't lost the spark at all. Not at their age. I figured they must be about 50 or 60 years old. And they looked fabulous. I administered their flu shots and commented on how wonderful they looked, but when I re-read their chart, I thought I was seeing things. The dates of birth didn't seem to add up.

They told me that they had been happily married for 62 years. That was wonderful! They looked more like 62 years of age rather than married for 62 years. I asked them what their secret was. The woman told me you can't afford to listen to negative people, because her friends and family never liked her husband when they first got married and said it wouldn't last. Well, there they were—62 happily wedded years later! Their friends and family had all passed on apparently. He was 92, and she was 88. I was shocked! They didn't look anywhere close to their ages.

They told me they don't dwell on their physical ages. In fact, they laughed that they forget how old they are and seek ways to enjoy their lives every single day. The golden couple also mentioned that their other secrets were eating right, being active, letting go of anger (never holding a grudge), injecting a dose of laughter into every day, counting their blessings, taking care of their health and checking in with their doctor regularly. They also shared with me that life was too full of stress and only the strong and the relaxed survive.

This Week's Hope Initiative:

Don't let your age be a deterrent from enjoying every aspect of your life. You're as old (or young!) as you feel. What ways can you work towards a life filled with hope and happiness?

Your Hopes for this Week:

_____

_____

_____

_____

Week 34:

Unleash Your Inner-Champion

*To be a champ is to believe in
yourself when no one else will.*

—Sugar Ray Robinson

School can be a challenge for any child at any level. But can you imagine sitting in a classroom trying to read a text and the words appear upside down or jumbled? How would you feel if you were teased by your peers and called "stupid" because of that and you could not understand why this was happening to you or why you could not see things the way others do?

This scenario describes dyslexia, a severe learning disability that impairs the ability to read. It can be devastating for any child. Jody, a young local woman, sent me her story to include in my newspaper column in 1995 detailing what she went through as a child in the school system before she was diagnosed with dyslexia.

She said she wanted her story to be shared with everyone to help any other child who may be going through the same condition or to parents of dyslexic kids, who feel frustrated because of their child's learning disability.

Jody said there were days when she felt alone and tearfully begged her mother to let her stay home from school. But after being tested and diagnosed, she was re-assigned to a special education class. Throughout her ordeal, she was told she would be lucky if she got through public school, let alone high school.

Well, today, Jody is a college graduate working full-time in her field of interest. Her message to others is that children with learning disabilities can learn, and don't tell them they can't.

It was through persistence, and a few caring teachers who helped her build her self-esteem, that she was able to push ahead and make the best of her situation.

She added if you know someone with a learning disability you shouldn't shun them because it's the worst thing you could do. Jody continues her crusade to inform and educate as she is often asked to address school assemblies on the subject of learning disabilities.

This Week's Hope Initiatives:

Is there some area of your life where you struggle? Believe in yourself and seek ways to overcome your challenges. Like Jody, never stop believing in yourself.

Your Hopes for this Week:

_____

_____

_____

_____

Week 35:

Perform Your Best Despite Calamity

Follow the 90/10 Principle: Life is 10% what
happens to you, 90% how you react to it.

—Author Unknown

Ever had one of those days at work where you feel as if you've been involuntarily cast as the lead character in a real life TV soap opera? You know, an episode full of dramatic mishaps, innuendos, conspiracy, misfortunes, where nothing goes right, people aren't what they appear and you're made to get on with the show anyway. Well, I remember having one of those days when I worked as an administrator many years ago. Trust me, it wasn't pretty—all the drama and never ending plot of a lead character without the prestige.

My day began when I got out of bed that morning. I was up late working on a freelance article. I woke up around 4:00 a.m. and went back to sleep, hit the buzzer on snooze at 6:00 a.m., but for some reason, my alarm didn't go off! So, I overslept! I dashed out the house, skin still moist from the shower, and hopped on the Go-train remembering that I had to be at the office before 8:00 a.m. for an early-rising client who wanted to meet with the executives. I barely made it. I literally tore around gathering necessities for the meeting. The coffee maker decided not to cooperate with me—it just wouldn't make the coffee. With a mind of its own, the photocopier thought it was a good time to suffer a nervous breakdown, and I had to prepare 40 double sided copies for the meeting. The fax machine jammed at the same time. My boss told me to look out for an urgent fax he was expecting for the meeting. The bell was ringing at the front desk. A courier demanded a signature for a package he was delivering. My colleague asked me for the report now, instead of next week as planned. The overhead projector light burned out. I went to make copies of the presentation but realized the copier still hadn't yet recovered from its breakdown. I looked bad, the company looked bad. And for the first time, I actually saw my career flash before my eyes.

Oh, on top of that, I glanced in the mirror to find out that the wind wasn't on my side that day either. My hair was neat when I left the house, but by the time I reached work, it looked as if I'd whisked it about with an egg-beater. My hair strands were pointing in every which direction but south. And it wasn't anywhere near 9:00 a.m. yet. Everyone was on to me to fix everything. I felt all of a sudden someone had unofficially designated this "Everything's-My-Fault-Day."

But then it dawned on me...what's the worst thing that could happen? I coaxed my hair back to its original polished coif. I was on the verge of tears until I remembered something someone had told me. Worry doesn't change anything, it just makes things *look* worse. Of course, I got out of the restroom and got on with the show. I even joked about the characteristics of the office machines....technology these days. I asked everyone to be patient while I looked into getting everything back in working order. I drew in a deep breath and did what I had to do. And you know something? The day turned out to be much better than I had visualized. I figured you can't let your circumstances change you. You must be the one to change your circumstances.

And by the way, there are a lot worse things that could happen than losing your job. For example, losing your self-respect or good health, just to name two! A former colleague of mine was battling illness, and it certainly put things into perspective about workplace stress. Don't let it get to you. It's not worth it. As it turned out, instead of being the recipient of rebuking at the end of the day for what had happened, the early morning client commented he appreciated people who handled stress well. He even told me he personally would have freaked out if he were in my position. "You certainly play your part well," he praised as he gave me a surreptitious wink.

This Week's Hope Initiative:

Think of ways of handling an unfavorable situation at work. It could be counting to ten (or one hundred if you must) to calm yourself down or it could mean thinking of ways out of the problem instead of dwelling on the problem itself.

Your Hopes for this Week:

_____

_____

_____

_____

Week 36:

Give Time: The Most Valuable Gift

We make a living by what we get. But we make a life by what we give.

—Sir Winston Churchill

It is good to help someone who can't return the favor, as someone once said. From a young age I was always taught about the values of giving. I learned later that you don't have to be rich to give or even make a difference. And time is the most valuable gift you can give. Volunteering is a great place to start. I've always thought it should be part of the curriculum in schools. I've learned a lot over the years:

Through the distress centre as a crisis intervention telephone counselor, I learned about the values of active listening. We really don't know how to listen empathetically without judgment or the urge to fill a void or offer advice. I gained valuable listening skills, honestly, a quality I never knew I lacked. In communication, listening is sometimes more powerful than talking.

Through a children's services organization as a case aide volunteer, I learned how important it is for children to have role models or people whom they can turn to. Spending time is more important than spending money where children are concerned.

Through the Jerry Lewis Labor Day Telethon for Muscular Dystrophy, as a telephone pledge-line volunteer, I was amazed by the other volunteers I had met. Some who have Muscular Dystrophy themselves. Many of them were born healthy but were stricken with the disease later in life. This taught me how much we take our good health for granted too often.

With the local District School Board-Adult Learning program, I volunteered as a literacy tutor for adults who were learning how to read and write. I wasn't aware that illiteracy was an invisible disability and many who are illiterate missed out on basic schooling when they were young for a variety of reasons. This made me realize how extremely important it is to read to your child starting at a young age. Illiterate adults are disadvantaged in that they can't understand simple instructions like guidelines on household products or job application forms, nor can they write directions for others or fill out medical forms. One of the saddest aspects is they are unable to read to their children! It is a privilege too many take for granted.

The more I go out into the community to volunteer is the more I see things differently, the more I see things we take for granted daily.

This Week's Hope Initiative:

If you are able to, why not donate some of your time to your local volunteer association? Even if your life is busy, like mine, you can opt to participate in short-term or one-time assignments. You will feel rewarded about helping those in need and as an added bonus you gain valuable insight and experience.

Your Hopes for this Week:

_____

_____

_____

_____

Week 37:

Take Responsibility for Your Actions

*The ability to accept responsibility is the
measure of the man.*

—Ray L. Smith

What would you do if you were in an embarrassing situation? Would you follow your conscience or your ego?

Years ago, while walking through the Toronto Eaton Center, my rather large handbag swung and knocked a small vase off a display shelf. The expensive vase smashed into pieces with an "in-stereo" sound crash that drew much attention from shoppers and store employees. Stunned and humiliated, my heart speeding 20 beats over the limit, I got down on my knees to pick up the scattered pieces. While I was down there, I prayed I wouldn't have to pay for it.

A friend who was with me at the time told me to leave it, that it was an accident. Dismayed at his statement I responded, "Just because it was an accident doesn't mean I'm not responsible. It was my handbag that knocked it over. Besides, someone could get hurt on these broken pieces." Not that I expected anyone to be walking barefoot through the Eaton's Department Store. We were already late for a meeting, so again he persisted. "They'll probably make you pay for it." "That's a chance I'll have to take," I replied. "It's the right thing to do. You don't just walk away from a mess." I then approached one of the cashiers. She seemed surprised to see me with the broken pieces. "Oh, you didn't have to, I was going to clean it up," she said casually, chewing gum.

My friend had then given me the old I-told-you-so-now-don't-you-feel-silly? look. But I maintained that regardless of the consequences, whether praise or punishment, if we all take responsibility for our actions and have unconditional respect for another's property, think of what a better society this would be.

This Week's Hope Initiative:

If you make a mess, clean it up. Sometimes it's that simple. Follow this simple rule if you find yourself in a puddle of trouble you single-handedly created.

Your Hopes for this Week:

_____

_____

_____

_____

Week 38:

Believe in the Power of Your Abilities

*All our dreams can come true, if we have
the courage to pursue them.*

—Walt Disney

The late, great R&B singer Aaliyah was only 15-years-old when I interviewed her for a story for the September, 1994 issue of *Word Magazine*. She was one of the very first recording artistes I interviewed early in my journalism career. She possessed 15 years of extraordinary talent, unlimited dedication, beauty and intelligence. I found her story quite remarkable. She told me she worked hard and always believed in herself. Despite having lost on Star Search in 1990 when she was only 11-years-old, the songbird never gave up. Just because one window of opportunity closes, there's always another one. She told me that being an entertainer was something she always wanted.

Aaliyah was also a straight A student at the Detroit School of the Performing Arts and always knew how to prioritize. She didn't let her artistic talents get in the way of a good education and working hard in school. She was intelligent beyond her years. So articulate, so wise.

She wasn't afraid to say that her true motivational force was her faith in God.

She also opined that sometimes people get what they want then they stop working hard. "But you've always got to work hard," she shared with me.

I enjoyed watching her dreams unfold into reality over the years following that interview. She worked tirelessly and was determined to expand her talents. Aaliyah had accomplished most of what she had set her heart and soul to do.

One trait I admired about her was her humility. She was very modest about her success at the time (as later) with her platinum single "Back and Forth" and her successful debut album. (She subsequently recorded several successful albums including the soundtrack to Dr. Dolittle and had scores of movie roles including Romeo Must Die, Queen of the Damned, and she was to have a part in the Matrix 2 and 3 before her untimely death.)

She had become an international superstar. Sadly, her tragic demise in a plane crash in August, 2001 ended her life at 22 years of age. But she had lived her life so fully by blessing others—that it was not in vain. As the then 15- year-old Aaliyah expressed during that interview to all those who have a career dream in their heart, "Go for what you feel. If I didn't try for this career, I would definitely regret it. I know I've always wanted this, and that's why I'm working towards this now. If you have a goal, go for it. At least try it. Don't regret it later."

This Week's Hope Initiative:

Is there a dream in your heart you've always wanted to chase but were too afraid to try? Make it a plan to reassess your goals and plan how to reach your dream. If there is an activity (hobby, talent, craft) that you would regret not attempting when you reach an older age, maybe it's time to take a look at that ambition.

Your Hopes for this Week:

_____

_____

_____

_____

Week 39:

Don't Be Discouraged; Be Determined

*The tests of life are not to break
you but to make you.*

—Author Unknown

Sometimes it's difficult to see the light in a dark situation, but that is when it is absolutely necessary. It was quite a few years ago but I still remember how I felt when I was a third year nursing student during the second SARS (Severe Acute Respiratory Syndrome) outbreak. I thought to myself this SARS thing is really back again, isn't it? News reports were in circulation of not only doctors and nurses injured through this ordeal on the job, but at least one nurse had gotten ill and died as a result of helping a SARS patient. This was tragic and discouraging at the same time for the nursing students and staff. But I was determined and had a strong desire to dedicate my life to saving others and assisting those with illnesses. I was asked if I still wanted to be a nurse despite the risks involved. The answer was a resounding YES!

I had to fight hard not to be discouraged. This was the second week since we became a level two hospital, and it was challenging for many of the students, workers and visitors to the hospital. Upon entering the facility, I felt as if I was on an assembly line rather than in a health care setting. The SARS screeners, much like the perfume lady at the department store, followed me around the table to squirt me with alcohol based hand sanitizer. Then I had to answer a questionnaire about my whereabouts and if I was at risk. My temperature was taken to ensure I didn't have a fever. Next up, I was given an N95 mask (like theirs) to protect me against the deadly, mysterious viral enemy without a face (that seemed to travel and attack people in mysterious ways). I was then given a yellow isolation gown to wear over my uniform. Finally, I was provided latex gloves and oversized goggles to use. I felt like I was wearing battle gear rather than a nursing uniform. Sweat began to pour down my face. I was tempted to lift the mask to catch my breath, but I was warned not to.

I had to get used to this quickly so that I could get on with my nursing care. But it seemed like a barrier. My throat felt dry and itchy. It was impossible to sneak sips of water without first finding the keys to the bathroom or staff lounge, the only places where the masks could come off temporarily. I guess, as they say, the only barrier we must overcome is in our minds.

After the morning shift change report, I gathered my necessary equipment to meet my patient, Mr. M., who was a cheery, 70-year-old man with an infection of the bone and neuropathic right foot ulcer. He had a below the knee amputation on his left leg.

I am always amazed at how people with the greatest ailments can have the greatest spirits to match. It is as if they find strength within to cope with the adversity they experience outside of themselves. Mr. M. was also diabetic with hypertension and other problems. But you would never know by speaking to him and laughing with him.

I was deeply touched by his bravery and his sentiments. He was determined to not be discouraged by having to be in the hospital during the outbreak. He was determined to keep his spirits up, and he told me he wanted to cheer up the staff and students who still came in to work risking their own lives to care for the patients. He was an unlikely source of inspiration, but he gave me an extra boost of courage to propel forward despite fear of the unknown. I tried to push the sorrow I felt for those medical professionals injured or deceased as a result of the outbreak to the back of my mind so that I could continue the work—their work. At the time, we didn't know how long the effect of this dreadful virus would last.

I had to wait until I was out of the hospital to actually take off the N95 mask, even after changing out of my uniform into street clothes. The bridge of my nose was swollen and sore from the tightness of the mask. My head was a little dizzy from breathing in all of my CO_2 while my nose and mouth had a distinctive round ring around it where the mask was positioned on my face.

This was clearly a reminder of the toil that frontline health care workers must go through while caring for others.

But it was that wonderful patient who was going through so much personal pain yet displayed so much courage with his illness who touched my life. His message was not to be discouraged. Be determined to pull through this in one spiritual peace.

No matter how terrible a storm may be, it will eventually come to pass.

This was a reminder there can be calmness during calamity. Soon after that shift, restrictions were lifted and the outbreak was contained. What got us through those times was visualizing an end to the ordeal, realizing that we cannot change a situation but only our attitudes towards it and determination to be resilient through this difficult period as we dealt with physical discomfort and fear of the unknown. The SARS episode made many of us nursing students stronger and prepared us in a strange way for the future as Registered Nurses.

This Week's Hope Initiative:

Regardless of your afflictions, try visualizing a positive outcome for whatever adverse situation you are in. Remember that storms never stay, they come to pass. A positive mind-set, determination, and courage can drive you to overcome any barrier.

Your Hopes for this Week:

_____

_____

_____

_____

Week 40:

Melt into Motherhood

Enjoy the little things in life, for one day
you may look back and realize they
were the big things.

—Author Unknown

It's never what happens, but how you interpret it that becomes your reality. Sure, my pregnancy wasn't the easiest in the world, but it was the most blessed. I realize this when I look back now. After my near-death experience days after giving birth to my lovely son, I never again looked at life the same way. Especially when I look into the innocent, glowing eyes of my dear young son.

I forget about the pregnancy challenges: the swollen ankles, puffy hands, water retention, hypertension, mood swings, stretch marks, nausea, and reflux.

Instead, I remember the swift, firm kicks within my womb to remind me that my baby was developing normally, feet shuffling inside of me, his heartbeat which sounded like a galloping horse during OB visits, his movements, stretching, wiggling, rotating inside of me, growing. All of this happening while I go about my daily activities. A precious miracle!

I forget about the backaches, bellyaches, headaches, frequent bathroom breaks, sleepless nights, and clothes too tight, worrying if baby inside me was alright. The weird cravings. The weight gain, pelvic pain, bladder urges, sugar surges, tons of tests, struggling to rest. The 16 hours of labor.

Instead, I remember the moment when he first came into the world. His father saw him first and cut the umbilical cord, taking an active role in his arrival. I remember the first time I held him when the nurse placed him on my chest, and the calmness of the delivery room.

I forget about the first few months of broken sleep, limited mobility, heightened sensitivity, constant fatigue from lack of solid sleep, and life in two or three hour intervals, changing diapers round the clock, feeding baby round the clock, sterilizing bottles around the clock, saline nose drops, bulb suctions, Gripe water, lugging heavy child car seats.

Instead, I remember the cuddles, the soothing, the playing, stimulating baby's senses, his first toothless smile, his warm touch. Being honored to provide for him, embrace him, protect him, nurture him, support him; believing in him, cherishing him, reading to him, singing to him. Holding him. Treasuring him. Unconditionally loving him.

When you see the beauty of each situation or take the time to appreciate the miracle and enjoy the smile of your child, everything else simply melts away.

This Week's Hope Initiative:

Love your child, unconditionally. Make a conscious decision to enjoy every blessed moment of raising your bundle of joy. Learn from the challenges but focus on the blessings.

Your Hopes for this Week:

_____

_____

_____

_____

Week 41:

Acquire a New Skill

Life is a progress, and not a station.

—Ralph Waldo Emerson

These days, as the job situation looks less than promising, many college students often wonder what to do. Go back to school and spend more money on education? Or master a new skill to add to your training?

I remember talking to a graduate with a master's degree who was working in a nursing home cleaning the floors. Every job is important, however, he told me that in obtaining his Masters degree in Philosophy he wished he had backed it up with other skills. He didn't have many practical job-related skills at the time to compete for certain jobs.

I also had a liberal arts degree in Psychology (my first degree) during a time when people were sporting t-shirts that read: "Hi, I have a degree from Harvard, would you like fries with that order?" We all had to create our own opportunities during competitive recession times. It was not just my degree that launched my first job out of university back in the early 90s, but a skill I learned in high school—the ability to accurately type 50-60 words per minute—that got me into an administrative job allowing me to put food on the table, before I went into jobs that focused on my education. (This was before I ventured into freelance writing for various newspapers, and later nursing, a job that I was inspired to do after volunteering my time visiting lonely patients.)

Since the average person has between 500 and 800 different skills and abilities, it's useful to take stock and inventories of what we are able to do from time to time. You never know what impact a simple skill you possess can have on your life or those around you.

One useful piece of advice I received in the past was from my Senior Public School principal, to learn something else. Learn a skill!

Don't just rely on textbook knowledge. That could be the difference between getting a job or missing out because of lack of experience.

Mr. Charlton's graduation anecdote about a well educated philosopher and an uneducated fisherman should be shared with all graduates—at all levels.

A philosopher and a fisherman sat in a boat on the lake. The philosopher with his PhD asked the uneducated fisherman if he knew anything about Plato or any of the great philosophers of the past.

The uneducated fisherman scratched his head and replied, "Nope. I know nothing about philosophy."

The philosopher with the PhD responded, "Do you realize that you've just lost a third of your life?" He then asked, "Do you know anything about literature and the great writings of our time?"

Again, the uneducated fisherman scratched his head and replied, "Nope. I know nothing about literature."

Dismayed, the philosopher with his doctorate training replied, "Do you realize that you've just lost two thirds of your life?"

Suddenly, the boat hit a sharp object and began to sink.

Now it was the uneducated fisherman who turned to the well-educated philosopher and said, "Excuse me, Mr. Philosopher, but the boat is sinking. Do you know how to swim?"

The educated philosopher shook his head in a panic and exclaimed, "No! I do not know how to swim. I never learned."

The fisherman then shook his head with regret as he replied to the philosopher, "Do you realize, sir, that you've just lost ALL of your life?"

This Week's Hope Initiative:

The bottom line is that school is a solid foundation we all need to succeed in this world. The better educated we are, the more we are able to enrich our own lives and increase our understanding. However, we must build ourselves up with practical skills, people skills and survival skills. We have the capability of up to 800 skills and abilities, so what are you waiting for?

Your Hopes for this Week:

_____

_____

_____

_____

Week 42:

Offer a Kind Word or Sweet Gesture

Good actions are never lost.

—Turkish Proverb

Caring people are the DNA of our community. They are the building blocks that keep our society in place. Think of what type of city we would live in if there were no Good Samaritans.

A few years ago, I witnessed an incident where a local youth stood with his backpack in between the doors of a TTC bus so the driver couldn't close the doors. He wasn't about to get on—he just looked off into the distance.

People were beginning to wonder why he was holding up their ride. They gazed disapprovingly at his appearance with his baggy pants hanging off his hips, sneakers and his braided hair.

"Maybe he's waiting for a friend," someone said. But moments later, we saw an elderly woman approach the bus smiling thankfully at him. She carried a walking stick and was barely able to walk, let alone run for the bus. She was the reason he held the door for her as she struggled to reach the bus.

He was holding it for her because he knew she wouldn't be able to catch up to the bus before the driver left the bus stop. He had run for the bus when he saw she was struggling to walk quickly towards the bus stop. Imagine that: going out of your way to help someone in need.

We should credit such young people who seem to go unnoticed until something negative happens.

While walking downtown on a busy afternoon some time ago, a homeless man glanced in my direction and smiled at my friend, Tony. "Hey you," he cried to Tony, "Thanks for the lunch."

"What was that about?" I inquired with a puzzled expression. As it turned out, earlier in the day the same man had begged Tony for some spare change. Wary about giving money for the reason that it may not go to wise use, Tony asked the man if he wanted something to eat. He said yes, so Tony bought him lunch, for which the homeless man was grateful. The idea is that a few dollars may be nothing to you, but it could mean everything to someone else. In this case, it meant buying another human being his first nutritious meal in days. This situation is commonly referred to as a random act of kindness. I know I've appreciated having doors opened for me when my arms were weighted down with bags of groceries.

These acts of kindness are not limited to strangers and passersby. We often overlook public service employees who go out of their ways to extend warm sentiments.

For example, the cab driver who carries you to your destination although you are short of the full fare, the bus driver who, although behind schedule, waits patiently as you run in the distance for the bus.

It's been said the trademark of a close-knit community is its caring people. It's how citizens are treated by one another. Perhaps if everyone did his or her part to help someone in need without expecting anything in return, society would be a much better place. What can you do today to offer a kind gesture to someone in need?

This Week's Hope Initiative:

Think of ways you can give someone a kind word or offer a sweet gesture. It could be as simple as opening a door for an elder or imparting a genuine compliment to someone who could use encouragement.

Your Hopes for this Week:

_____

_____

_____

_____

Week 43:

Strive for Excellence and Nobility

We need to internalize this idea of excellence.
Not many folks spend a lot of time trying to be excellent.

—U.S. Senator Barack Obama

In 1994, I wrote a two-part feature story titled the Fountain of Achievement: An Endless Flow of Positive Role Models for an ethnic newspaper. Positive role models are not always covered in the news, so from this vastly running fountain of achievement, I managed to scoop up a cup of successful young people from varied backgrounds and proffer their advice to other youth. They all shared a similar formula for success: hard work + dedication + perseverance = achievement. I also noticed they shared a burning desire to give back to their communities.

I interviewed Andy, a young barber, who at 17 while still in high school set up his own hairstyling business. The self-motivated youth had a strong clientele. He called it the art of making people look great. What I found remarkable was that he never hesitated to share his skills with friends and help them to set up businesses for themselves. Guided by faith in God, he told me that giving thanks to the Lord is a routine that never slipped with him.

Michelle, a 29-year-old real estate vice president of Silwin Real Estate whose habit of self-discipline and motivation cultivated while growing up, enabled her to be the Ontario Champion of Public Speaking at age 12. She started teaching ballet and jazz at Maureen Stuart School of Dancing at age 15 while maintaining straight A's in school. At the age of 18 while completing high school, she received her Real Estate Practitioner's License. When most of her peers were out having fun, she remembered owning her first property by the time she was 20 and having a mortgage to pay. She now holds an honors degree in Economics and Management and has collected many prestigious awards. Michelle told me she was "never in competition with anyone" but herself and "perseverance is the key."

I then spoke with Anthony, who at 17 years was a published writer and had been an entertainment journalist for a local newspaper having interviewed Queen Latifa, Patti Labelle, and RUN DMC among others. The young journalist advocated that "education is a must." He admitted that without his "supermom," Dorett, he would be nothing. "My mother taught me my self-worth, self-pride, self-respect and to be proud of myself and my heritage and what I stand for." She is a strong single parent, whose words stood by him. "Know where you want to go and don't let anyone tell you that you can't because of your age, color, sex or race. Have inner peace and self-control and you'll succeed."

I also interviewed Mitzie, who, at 22, was working 14 hour days as the president of her own model and talent agency with two divisions. She later went into producing fashion shows after realizing the gross misrepresentation of women of color by establishing employment within the modeling sector. She actively controlled events management, production of fashion shows and various social and fundraising events. The U of T graduate had been president of the Student's Administrative Council and dedicated her time to helping other youths in the community. Additionally, she organized the first Cultural Awareness Week for the city and was the editor of a community newspaper and the director and coordinator for Club 65 which provided activities for more than 250 local senior citizens. She believed it was important to "always be in touch with reality." Her parents, too, were hard working entrepreneurs. She continues to serve her community on the boards of several organizations, including TV Ontario, United Way of Greater Toronto, Yonge Street Mission, Housing Services Inc., and Emerging Leaders Network, where she co chairs the Leadership Summit. She subsequently became editor of several publications, president of SMART Toronto, a leading association for high technology industries, and is presently the vice president, external affairs and corporate secretary for Goodwill. Mitzie completed her Executive MBA at Rotman School of Management at the University of Toronto.

I interviewed a young artist, Robert Small, who used art to promote cultural awareness. He captured the spirit of life and the emotions and recreated them in the form of art with his experience as an artist and businessman. The then 24-year-old university graduate illustrated images of the African Canadian Diaspora experience. Small was then president of Exodus Images, an editorial cartoonist, office manager for Black Pages and a published writer. "Setting goals for yourself and striving to reach heights" are important he told me. He also explained that his future aspirations were to increase his activity in the community, bring his art to a national scale and pursue a law degree. Today, he owns his own art gallery and has become a significant artist in Canadian history. He presented his artwork to former Canadian Prime Minister Jean Chretien. Small told me in the interview that "regardless of your obstacles, always remain confident in yourself." He continues to chronicle the achievements of notable African-Canadians with the annual release of a poster celebrating Black History Month called LEGACY.

This Week's Hope Initiative:

Ask yourself what you are doing for your community and those around you. Are you working to your greatest potential? Do you strive to excel at your chosen profession? Are you setting a good example? Are you living life to the fullest? Are you using your skills to not only work but to help others in a sincere way?

Your Hopes for this Week:

_____

_____

_____

_____

Week 44:

Learn from Historical Figures

Most of the important things in the world have been accomplished by people who have kept trying when there seemed to be no hope at all.

—Dale Carnegie

I attended my younger sister's graduation from Mary Shadd Public School. After glancing over at the monument in the lobby of the school, I was stunned to realize that in the 1800s not only was Mary Shadd Canada's first female reporter, editor and publisher, but she was a black woman!

Amidst the hardships of slavery, sexism and the trials of being a woman and black in a time when the rights of those two groups were almost nonexistent—a time when all the odds were stacked up against her—Shadd became a school teacher, principal, lecturer, women's rights' activist and the first female law student at Howard University in the U.S.

She became a lawyer at the age of 60 as well. A remarkable accomplishment even by today's standards. Shadd was a woman who believed that in most cases the future lies in our own hands. Knowledge is power, and we must strive to accomplish more every day, no matter what our circumstances.

She had learned a great deal from her father who had pioneered the underground railroad, and she instilled the same values in her two children. Widowed at a young age, she left the U.S. with the responsibility of being a single parent, while lobbying for the rights of women and slaves.

Although she graced the planet for only 70 years, dying in 1893, her story today brings many of us hope and motivation to move ahead and accomplish great deeds. She didn't let being black or female stop her from achieving her dreams or limit her courage to fight for a better world. For more information on inspiring profiles, visit the Ontario Black History Society's website at www.blackhistorysociety.ca.

This Week's Hope Initiative:

What can you learn from Shadd's experience? What's stopping you from accomplishing your goals and making your dreams a reality?

Your Hopes for this Week:

_____

_____

_____

_____

Week 45:

Don't Squander Time

Time is the most valuable thing a man can spend.

—Diogenes Laertius

"Every second counts," opined our pastor at rehearsal. Of course, he was directing this message to us, a group of amateur actors, as we practiced for the church Christmas play in 1999, One Holy Night.

At this time of the year, we've all got our commitments, ranging from family gatherings, holiday preparations and work functions, to hopping around town for Christmas sales and the midnight madness rush. Most of us would agree that in terms of socializing, December is the most hectic or stressful social month of the year.

As our young pastor suggested, time is extremely valuable and should be spent wisely. Not because we were doing something special by taking part in a drama with a powerful message about forgiveness and faith, but as he said, we were giving freely of our time for a good cause.

This reminded me of Christmas, 1999—the last in the century and millennium. As we thought about what to buy for our loved ones (and how we'd be struggling to pay for it in the next millennium), we were reminded that time is the most valuable and irreplaceable gift we could give a person.

We needed to ask ourselves if we had taken the time to be grateful for what we had by showing our appreciation to our significant others.

Had we taken the time to sit down and listen to someone close to us? Had we taken the time to really love someone? To show someone we cared by doing fun activities with them, or call them or write an encouraging message in a Christmas card?

As I penned my last column for the millennium, I couldn't help but muse at how quickly time had slipped through my fingers.

For instance, it had already been five years since I wrote my first column for the *Mirror*. During that time, I had set many five-year goals I didn't get to follow-up on, ranging from doing more volunteer work and spending more time on the stuff that I cherish with the people I care about. But as one philosopher phrased it, time waits for no one.

Though some skeptics would disagree, I believe our generation is actually the most fortunate to have witnessed something that won't happen for another 1,000 years—the turning of the millennium.

So as we stocked up on our canned foods, bottled water and candles (just in case things weren't Y2K compliant and didn't function at the stroke of midnight on December 31, 1999), I wrote about how we should also remember the aspects that will always be compliant—regardless of the year or century, like love, happiness, and closeness to family and friends.

And since time seems to be the one entity that is wasted more than food in this part of the world, I wanted to share a message (a famous poem by an unknown author) that was e-mailed to me by a colleague regarding the value of time:

To realize the value of one year, ask a student who has just failed a final exam.

To realize the value of one month, ask the mother who has given birth to a premature baby.

To realize the value of one week, ask an editor of a weekly newspaper.

To realize the value of one day, ask a general laborer who has seven mouths to feed.

To realize the value of one hour, ask the lovers who are waiting to meet.

To realize the value of one minute, ask the person who has just missed the train, bus or plane.

To realize the value of one second, ask the person who has survived an accident.

To realize the value of one millisecond, ask the athlete who has won the silver medal in the Olympics.

Time waits for no one. Yesterday is history. Tomorrow is a mystery. Today is a gift. That's why it's called the present.

This Week's Hope Initiative:

Treasure every moment you have. Share your moments with someone special.

Your Hopes for this Week:

_____

_____

_____

_____

Week 46:

Live Life to the Fullest in Preparation for the Unknown Future

*Life is not measured by the number of breaths
we take but by the number of moments
that take our breath away.*

—Author Unknown

It has been said that it's not the time you have left but how you spend your time that counts. I can't help but direct my thoughts back to Mrs. Smith when I think about that saying. She was a friend of the family who passed away a number of years ago from breast cancer. She was always regarded as a colorful, high-spirited person who loved and lived life to the fullest. She did not let her diagnosis of cancer prevent her from living in the moment.

I remember the conversation we had just a few weeks before she died. She always maintained her grace and willingness to offer kind words—even during the last few weeks of her life. She told me that too many people take life for granted.

She said that looking back with regrets is the worst thing you can do when the end is near, so you must follow your dreams.

Mrs. Smith told me that regret was not something in her spiritual diet. She enjoyed going places and spending time with friends before her illness and still maintained her activities towards the end. She spoke vibrantly of the things in life that gave her joy, her travels around the world and her outlook on life. She said she did not look back with sorrow because she lived her life fully. The way she wanted to live it. She was satisfied with her life. She was one of the first people

I had spoken to who knew she had limited time left but lived it with purpose and in good spirits. Many of us waste time on petty worries or frivolities, but those who know the value of how limited time is seem to cherish every moment they have as a gift.

Little did she know that her inspiring words changed my outlook on life. A couple of years after I spoke to her, I would also later join the family tradition of health care and study nursing, later specializing in the care of cancer patients.

April is Cancer Awareness Month, and although breast cancer is found mostly in women, men have a very small chance of developing breast cancer, particularly later in their lives. As the Canadian Cancer Society states: "Early detection is the best method for saving lives." They say that the earlier you start the screening process, the better. For more information about cancer, support services, research and prevention, visit the Canadian Cancer Society at *www.cancer.ca.*

As Mrs. Smith commented, we need to live each moment as a precious gift, that's what the present is all about. It's not about living in the past or worrying about the future. Nor is it about taking anything for granted. It's about achieving our dreams and valuing our time.

This Week's Hope Initiative:

A song titled Live Like You Were Dying, says it all. Powerful. Moving. Encouraging. Live your dreams. Enjoy your moments. Every blessed one of them. Be inspired. Also, visit YouTube.com and view the Last Lecture: Really Achieving your Childhood Dreams, a powerfully, uplifting 76-minute inspirational lecture given by a brave and vibrant, (then) dying 47-year-old professor by the name of Randy Pausch or pick up his book titled The Last Lecture. You will never view life the same way again.

Your Hopes for this Week:

_____

_____

_____

_____

.

Week 47:

Rise after a Disgraceful Fall

You cannot control what happens to you, but you can control your attitude towards what happens and in that you will be mastering change rather than letting it master you.

—Brian Tracy

You may remember the Patti Starr affair some years back. Well, from former political insider and fundraiser to being referred to as Canada's answer to Danielle Steel, she came a long way. And it wasn't easy.

I interviewed Starr in 1995 for my *Perspectives* column. "When my world was demolished five years ago, I had no choice," Starr said of her rise and fall in the political arena. "I had to try to make a life. Fortunately for me, I met Jack Stoddard who published Tempting Fate, which was the story of what happened from my perspective."

Starr said it was so well reviewed that he gave her the opportunity to present her manuscript of fiction. The mother of five, who said she has learned to put the past behind her and focus on the present wants to be known as a writer. A novelist.

But Starr's comeback can certainly be viewed as a learning experience for anyone. Today, she owns her own business.

Similarly, I had written an article on Vanessa Williams, the former Miss America, for an ethnic newspaper. Her story of revamping her image after losing her crown following a scandal is remarkable. She focused on her gifts and talents and moved on.

This Weeks Hope Initiatives:

I created a list of some intriguing lessons from adages that we can all find useful:

1. *Don't be the guest of honor at your own pity party. You can either curl up in a corner or learn from a bad experience and move on.*

2. *The only person who never makes a mistake is the one who does absolutely nothing. Don't be afraid to do something.*

3. *Obstacles are those frightening things you see when you take your eyes off your goals. Never take your eyes off your goals.*

4. *Ideas are funny things. They don't work unless you do. You can have great dreams and aspirations, but it's only a dream if you don't get to it and work to materialize it.*

5. *The Pope (John Paul) once said that "people should never be ashamed to say they have been wrong, which is saying, in other words, they are wiser today than yesterday."*

Remember the saying: The largest room in the world is the room for improvement.

Your Hopes for this Week:

_____

_____

_____

_____

Week 48:

Know What's Best for You: Take Inventory of Your Life

Whatever you are, be a good one.

—Abraham Lincoln

Many of us are beginning to take a second look at investing in our future. Enjoying life to the fullest and being the best that we can be is ideal.

In 1995, I interviewed Mariel Camilleri of the Apex Centre (now owner of Mysthaven Country Retreat & Spa just north of Toronto) who specializes in success coaching. She said there are countless ways to be the best you can be with many different approaches to reaching your goal.

"Although success means different things to different people, the levels that people are making changes are on physical, emotional, mental and spiritual. All those ways of self-development can help you be more in touch with what's important to you, thereby creating more of the results that are available to you," said Camilleri.

Common complaints that show up in school, work, or other areas of our lives tend to evoke the responses: "I'm not happy in my job," "I'm not managing my time well," or "I don't really know what I want."

To be effective and create the life you want, Mariel offered some helpful tips in that article which included taking charge of your life. I've included this advice with this week's hope initiatives.

This Week's Hope Initiatives:

1. *Ask yourself what's really important to you. Reflect on your values, your likes, your dislikes and what is good for your overall well-being. Don't try to be like anyone else. Be you.*

2. *Ask yourself what's standing in the way of where you'd like to be. Create a plan to get there.*

3. *Ask yourself how you can manifest that personal vision in your life to fulfill your purpose for being.*

4. *Work smart, not hard. The majority of time we spend is spent on time wasters. We should eliminate these and concentrate on what's important.*

5. *She added that there are three types of activities that take up time: 1) Priorities: things that are important to us; 2) Obligations: things that are important to those who are important to us; and 3) Time wasters: things that take up valuable time, such as daydreaming, shuffling papers, etc.*

6. *Focus on what is important to you and direct your energy on that goal.*

7. *Exercise regularly. A healthy mind and body go hand in hand.*

8. *Eat healthy. You are what you eat, as the saying goes.*

9. *Be realistic with your goals. The key is knowing what is best for you.*

Your Hopes for this Week:

_____

_____

_____

_____

Week 49:

Reach out to those in Need

*The measure of life, after all is not in its
duration but its donation.*

—Peter Marshall

I remember one November, when the clock had been set back one hour, days were getting shorter and the temperatures were dropping. When the radio-alarm clock sounded, the on-air disc jockey announced that winter was coming. It was only November, I thought, and already the wind chill factor made it feel as if it was below zero degrees Celsius. As I woke up in the morning, the frosty air bit me hard. The heat in the house was turned down, and I struggled to get out of bed with the covers wrapped around me. But I didn't want to climb out of bed, let alone go outside.

After complaining about the house while turning up the thermostat, another cold reality hit me: the fact that there are thousands of people living on the streets of our city. They have nowhere to call home. They have no heat to complain about. They swallow a bitter cold dose of reality every day. Many die on the streets they call home.

Could you imagine what it would be like to live outdoors in bus shelters, inside doorways or on park benches? To many of us, it is unthinkable, or as we would like to think, unlikeable. But anyone can be homeless. For some, it's just a paycheck away.

It's worth noting, however, that many of the homeless are just like us. Many have jobs, but because they are low-paying jobs that barely cover basic rent in the city let alone food and transportation costs, they end up living in shelters.

In the article, I wrote that according to estimates, close to 10,000 homeless people live in the city. Unfortunately, many also live the harsh reality of having a pavement for a bed. But there have been great efforts from various organizations, including churches and schools, to donate warm clothes and nonperishable foods to the needy. Project Warmth (PW), for example, is an organization in Toronto that collects and distributes sleeping bags and warm clothing for the homeless. When I spoke to Peter Burns for that story, who at the time was one of the PW volunteer board members, his greatest concern was that people may not think about giving as much when the weather is warm. Before Christmas peeks around the corner, we should lend our support. It's always difficult during a blizzard to receive an outpouring (though appreciated), but it's better to prepare ahead of time in the event of unpredictable weather.

This Week's Hope Initiative:

If you have extra sleeping bags in good condition, or if you can spare some blankets for the needy, you can visit your local Goodwill or Salvation Army to donate. You can also make monetary donations to organizations such as the United Way of Canada 1-800-267-8221 or United Way of America 1-703-836-7112.

Your Hopes for this Week:

_____

_____

_____

_____

Week 50:

Tap into Your Available Resources

Create lists to remind you of what support you may have available to you. Take inventory of your life and the things that are important to you. Use lists as reminders to enjoy yourself and cultivate the various areas in your life from family to friends, recreational and support networks. For any lists that are empty, think of ways you can enhance your life by adding to them. For the family and friends list, those who you can turn to for support, remind them that you too are there for them in their time of need. Relationships work best when reciprocated.

SUPPORT NETWORKS:

My Support Network of Family:

My Support Network of Close Friends I can call upon in times of need:

Day Care Centers/ Schools for Children:

My Place of Worship:

Doctors/Medical Professionals/ Local Pharmacist:

Necessary Telephone Numbers:

Emergency: 911

Poison Control: 416-813-5900

Health Hotline: Telehealth Ontario   1-866-797-0000

The Distress Center   416-408-HELP (4357)

For activities, when you're feeling down or at a loss for events in which to engage, try referring to your list. Was there a movie that made you laugh aloud? Maybe it's time to pull it off the shelf or rent it and play it in your DVD player.

ACTIVITIES:

Things I enjoy doing (including activities with your children, your spiritual retreat and other ways to relax):

My Favorite Movies (or Television Shows):

My Favorite Books:

My Favorite Restaurants:

My Movies to See:

My Books to be Read:

Social Clubs/ Activity Clubs (including sports clubs, crafts clubs, Parent-Teacher-Association or online forums):

My Favorite Places to Shop:

My Favorite Places to Buy Gifts or Order Flowers (for instance, Tidy's in Toronto delivers flowers):

My Favorite Exercise Pastime:

Other Resources:

Week 51:

Personal Journal of Hope

Fill out the examples below (and make copies) for the coming weeks ahead. Reflect on all the goodness occurring in your life. Embrace the joyful moments. Learn from discouraging moments. In the future, you can re-read your journal entries and allow it to serve as a reminder to reflect on the personal growth journey in your life.

Date: _____

I'm thankful for: _____

My Hopes for today:

_____

_____

_____

_____

_____

_____

My Hope Action Plan:

_____

_____

_____

_____

_____

_____

Date: _____

I'm thankful for: _____

My Hopes for today:

_____

_____

_____

_____

_____

_____

_____

_____

_____

My Hope Action Plan:

_____

_____

_____

_____

_____

_____

_____

_____

_____

Date: _____

I'm thankful for: _____

My Hopes for today:

_____

_____

_____

_____

_____

_____

_____

_____

My Hope Action Plan:

_____

_____

_____

_____

_____

_____

_____

_____

_____

Week 52:

Record Your Blessings

Fill out the journal entries for the coming weeks ahead. List all the blessings in your life from the simple to the divine. Reflect on all the goodness happening to you or for you. Review this list every morning and add to it as you go along. Let this serve as a reminder for you during your discouraging moments that the glass is half full not half empty. Never stop counting your blessings everyday.

Date: _____

My blessings:

_____

_____

_____

_____

_____

_____

_____

_____

_____

_____

_____

_____

_____

Bonus Week:

Nurture Your Relationships

"The only way to have a friend is to be one."
—Ralph Waldo Emerson

Record a list of people you can send an encouraging or funny e-mail to once in a while:

Name   E-mail Address:

_____   _____

_____   _____

_____   _____

_____   _____

_____   _____

_____   _____

_____   _____

_____   _____

_____   _____

_____   _____

_____   _____

_____   _____

Record a list of people you can send a Christmas card or Holiday greeting to:

Name   Address:

_____   _____

_____   _____

_____   _____

_____   _____

_____   _____

_____   _____

_____   _____

_____   _____

_____   _____

_____   _____

_____   _____

_____   _____

_____   _____

_____   _____

_____   _____

_____   _____

_____   _____

_____   _____

_____   _____

Record a list of people you can call to brighten up their day once in a while:

Name   Telephone number:

_____   _____

_____   _____

_____   _____

_____   _____

_____   _____

_____   _____

_____   _____

_____   _____

_____   _____

_____   _____

_____   _____

_____   _____

_____   _____

_____   _____

_____   _____

_____   _____

_____   _____

_____   _____

Record a list of people you can send a birthday wish to, including family and close friends:

January

_____

_____

_____

_____

February

_____

_____

_____

_____

March

_____

_____

_____

_____

April

_____

_____

_____

_____

May

_____

_____

_____

_____

June

_____

_____

_____

_____

July

_____

_____

_____

_____

August

_____

_____

_____

_____

September

October

November

December

Record a list of places you can visit or fun activities you can do with your children, family and/or close friends. It could be visiting an amusement park, watching a movie, playing a game, taking a trip or simply doing arts and crafts together.

Activity	Location	With Whom?